# ClustERPuck

# ClustERPuck

## 21 Critical
## ERP Implementation
## Mistakes

*...and what to do instead!*

**SHANE WILLIAMS**

A catalogue record for this book is available from the National Library of Australia

First published in 2024 by Hambone Publishing
Melbourne, Australia

Editing by Mish Phillips, Laura McCall and Felicity Harrison
Interior design by David W. Edelstein

For information about this title, contact:
Shane Williams
shane@shanewilliams.com.au
shanewilliams.com.au

ISBN 978-0-6451617-2-4 (paperback)
ISBN 978-0-6451617-3-1 (ebook)
ISBN 978-0-6451617-4-8 (audiobook)

*For Kelly.*

On any given day of the year, it's summer somewhere in the world. Thank you for your unwavering encouragement and support as we build towards our 'Endless Summer', sharing experiences as we search the world for the perfect moment which may be waiting just over the horizon.

# Contents

## PART 2: IMPLEMENTATION

## PART 2A: YOU AND YOUR TEAM

## PART 2B: THE FINAL GRIND

# Introduction

Hey! Thanks for picking up my book. I thought I'd begin by just calling out the elephant in the room: Enterprise Resource Planning (ERP) is not a sexy topic. In fact, the only people who get enthusiastic about ERP are the folks who are selling ERP. The rest of us are just along for the journey. So, if you fall into the first camp and you're an enthusiast, welcome to the book. I hope you get some value. But if you're not in that camp, which I imagine is the majority of people who will read this book, then chances are that while you don't love ERP, you've come to the realisation that you need it.

I know you've got a lot on your plate. As a leader or business owner, every decision you make is critical – not just for the health of your business, but for your reputation and the livelihoods of your team. You've worked hard to get where you are, and the last thing you can afford is a misstep, especially when it comes to something as fundamental as the systems that run your company. That's a weight that can't be ignored, and I don't take that lightly.

Since you're reading a book about ERP implementations, it's likely you're at a particular stage in your business's growth. Most Small to Medium Enterprise (SME) manufacturing businesses follow a fairly typical journey through three stages.

**Growth**

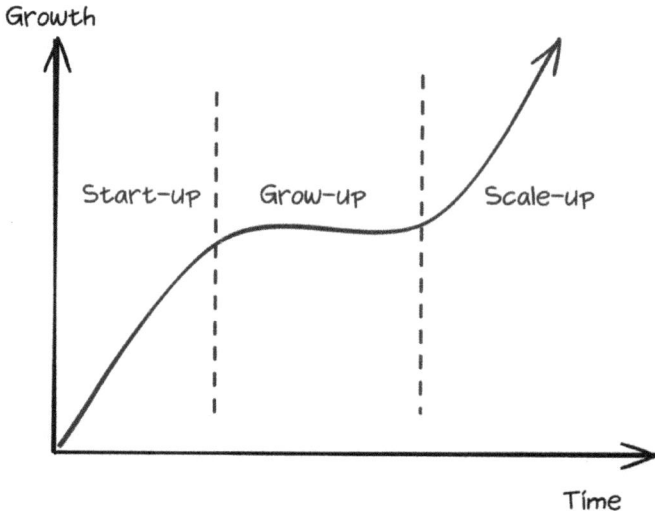

I call stage one the **start-up stage**. The business begins small, with a limited number of products, and you take them to market. The technology that supports you is probably no more than email and a small business finance system. But over time, as your business has grown, so too has the number of processes and people. Along with those come a raft of different technologies designed to solve various problems in your business. This could be a number of really complicated spreadsheets or a plethora of different bespoke systems, like time sheeting, inventory management, HR, warehousing, logistics, product configuration, etc. Perhaps it's all of the above.

The promise behind these technologies is simple - growth. Yet as you've likely found, the reality can be different. While opportunities lie ahead, the tools and processes you rely on often start to become barriers rather than enablers. Once you reach this tipping point, you're in what I call the **grow-up stage** - where the growing pains begin. This is where ERP starts to become a serious consideration for many businesses. If that sounds like where you are now, then you're in the right place. My goal is to help you get through these growing pains and into the **scale-up stage**.

I get it - the frustration of feeling like you're ready to take your business to the next level, but the systems you've relied on for so long are suddenly holding you back. You've built something great, but now every step forward feels like wading through mud. You're ambitious, capable, and committed to growth, but it's tough to feel confident when the technology meant to support your business becomes a bottleneck. If that sounds familiar, you're not alone - and that's exactly why I wrote this book.

Navigating out of this stage is where things get difficult. The incentives for sellers and buyers are misaligned. While you're looking for the minimum amount of technology to get through the growing pains and keep moving your business forward in a cost-effective manner, the folks who are selling you the solutions are motivated differently. If you haven't been on this journey before and don't know what you need, then you'll either make a decision to do nothing or jump in blindly, trust the salesman, and hope for the best.

Imagine embarking on a grand voyage with the promise of reaching a paradise where efficiency and productivity reign supreme, only to find yourself stranded in a chaotic wasteland, burning time and money while achieving none of your goals. This is the reality for many businesses that take the plunge into implementing ERP systems without proper preparation and guidance. Welcome to the world of the **ClustERPuck** – a term I've coined to describe these failed or suboptimal ERP implementations that often leave companies worse off than they started.

**ClustERPuck** (noun)

*Clust·ER·Puck | \ 'klʌstər͵pʌk *

1.  **Definition:** A suboptimal or abandoned ERP (Enterprise Resource Planning) implementation, often resulting from multiple errors or missteps during the selection and implementation phases, leading to significant inefficiencies, disruptions, and increased costs.
2.  **Usage:** 'Their ERP project turned into a ClustERPuck due to poor planning and lack of stakeholder involvement.'
3.  **Origin:** A portmanteau of 'clusterfuck' and 'ERP', illustrating the chaotic and problematic nature of a mismanaged ERP implementation.

Having witnessed the multitude of ways an ERP implementation can go wrong, I decided it was time to compile these lessons into a comprehensive guide. These insights are not solely from my own experiences but are also sourced from a vast array of industry experts and business owners who've worn the path before you. This book is for business leaders who want to avoid the pitfalls that turn an ERP dream into a ClustERPuck nightmare.

In the chapters that follow, I'll take you through the most common mistakes made during ERP projects and, more importantly, how to avoid them. From lack of leadership buy-in and underestimating internal effort, to over-customisation and misunderstanding the cost model, we'll cover the gamut of issues that can derail your ERP implementation. And because I don't want you to mess up, each chapter comes packed with real-world case studies, practical advice, and actionable strategies to help you navigate the ERP landscape successfully.

You might find the tone of this book a bit different from the typical corporate writing you're used to. That's intentional. I wanted to keep it real and engaging, much like a conversation you might have over a beer with a trusted advisor. Expect some frank language and direct advice - because sugar-coating the truth doesn't help anyone.

You'll notice that some of the chapters are different lengths. That's also deliberate. Some of the problems discussed are nuanced and require more in-depth exploration, while others are relatively straightforward. Each chapter is designed to give you just the right amount of information you need to understand the issue and take action.

So, whether you're about to embark on your ERP journey or are already in the thick of it and looking for a lifeline, **this book is for you**. Let's dive in and make sure your ERP implementation is a success story, not another ClustERPuck.

# The Shortcut

This book doesn't have an executive summary because it is, in and of itself, an executive summary. It's the shortest possible way I can convey the critical, but all-too-common mistakes SME manufacturers make trying to select and implement an ERP.

So, rather than 'executive summary', the title of this chapter is 'the shortcut' because inevitably, there's going be people reading this who fall into one of three categories:

1. You don't have the time to read a book and take in the learnings. You've got a busy schedule and just want to get things done.
2. You're going to delegate this, so you don't really need to know the details. You just need the Reader's Digest version so you can sound smart and tell other folks what to do.
3. You don't want to fuck it up, and you're actually ready to read the entire book.

If you fall into one of the first two categories, then screw all the advice in the latter pages of this book – you don't need it. Let's just cut to the chase.

The whole reason this book exists is because folks skipped one or several of the lessons in this book. Not to suggest that those people were stupid or lazy – they didn't have this book – so I'm giving them the benefit of the doubt that they weren't trying to take a shortcut and just didn't know. They're all smart people in successful businesses, and they've been kind enough to share their mistakes so you don't need to make them.

But unlike them, you can't claim ignorance if you take the shortcut and it goes to custard. You're holding the resource they never had. So, rather than preach to you, let me paint a picture of exactly where you're headed if you take the shortcut.

Focused on the perceived problem that's right in front of you, you'll go out and talk to a bunch of sales folks. They'll either prey on your *naïveté* to extract as much money as they can out of you, or they'll sell you something that they genuinely think will work for you, but only because you've told them the wrong problem. You'll also probably buy the one with the most bells and whistles because, hey, it seems like it's going to solve all of your problems – the Silver Bullet. Then the vendor's delivery team is going to come in and dutifully try to drag you across the line to get this thing installed. But, because you're taking a shortcut, you won't make the time, you won't dedicate the right people, you'll make it an extra duty on top of somebody's job, and you'll only do the bare minimum and get only half of what you actually need documented. Then your vendor will go away and build your ERP as you described.

What you're going to get is something that does what you told them it should do, but doesn't do what you need it to do, and probably is worse than what you've already got despite the fact that its whole purpose was to make things better. Then the narrative among you and your team will be that it's everybody's fault but yours. You never really took ownership of this problem in the first place; you took the shortcut, yet somehow this whole ClustERPuck will be the vendor's fault. They didn't listen. They didn't understand. They didn't build it right. Every industry event you turn up to, you'll shit-can the software and the folks who implemented it. You'll tell everyone to avoid it. You'll end up in this half-pregnant state where you've still got the old tools running, even though you're also using the new ones. Your staff will become more pissed off than they were before. Some of them will leave, and some will refuse to use the new tools. You'll be burdened with the cost of a software licensing agreement for multiple years, and you'll never achieve any of the bells and whistles that were promised because you first needed to get the basics right – and you won't ever be able to get that now. You'll end up burning a shit-tonne of money for absolutely no reward. In fact, you'll have made things worse. But don't worry – it'll be everybody else's fault but yours.

So if that sounds like a good idea, put the book down, burn it, throw it out, delete it if you're reading the ebook – I don't care. But please don't call me.

If you're willing tc reconsider, then maybe there's hope; the amount of time it's going to take you to read this book will be a blip on the radar compared to the amount of time you're going to spend digging yourself out of a hole when you screw it up.

In summary, if you're in camps 1 or 2 and can't be fucked doing the work, then just don't bother with an ERP. It's a waste of your time and money.

If you're in camp 3 and don't want to fuck it up – **welcome to my guide to avoiding a ClustERPuck.**

# PART 1

# PREPARATION

MISTAKE
1

# Not knowing what you REALLY need

THIS MISTAKE HAS multiple facets, but at its core, it boils down to not fully understanding what your business really needs, both now and in the future. When people start the process of finding a solution, they tend to focus only on the problems they have right now. For example, they might be dealing with issues in accounts receivable (AR) and accounts payable (AP), time sheeting, calculating the cost of goods, operational efficiency on the manufacturing floor, or supply chain problems. These immediate challenges drive them to look for a product that can solve those issues. While this seems reasonable and logical, it's a short-term fix.

**First**, focusing on immediate problems without considering future needs means that once you've solved your current issues and created capacity in your business, you'll start to run faster. You'll want to sell more products and serve more customers. A business that's now running faster will encounter new challenges. You'll need or want to create new capabilities or scale up existing ones. For example, you may never have had a sophisticated sales team with marketing automation capabilities because you were barely keeping up with the sales you already had. But now that you've solved many of your manufacturing and supply chain issues and can get invoices out quicker, you want to sell more. When you put in your ERP system, you focused on your current problems, and now you don't have the right solution for the business you're becoming.

**Second**, not knowing what you need can lead to buying a product based on features. For instance, you might start looking for a solution to your back-office finance and HR challenges, but without a deep understanding of your broader requirements, you could be sold on the virtues of automated online marketing or some other cutting-edge technology. It seems great, but in reality, it has little chance of being leveraged. Many of these high-value capabilities require a solid foundation in place, so you might end up paying a lot for features you can't use, that don't solve your actual problems.

**Third**, if you aren't clear on what's most important, you risk picking a product that doesn't fit your business. Research shows that many SMEs struggle with ERP implementations because the chosen system doesn't align with their specific business strategy. Every ERP system has its own strengths and weaknesses – a unique DNA. For instance, one vendor's ERP might be best in class for finance and have state-of-the-art reporting. However, it might not be particularly strong for complex inventory or managing engineering functions. If your business revolves around inventory or product design but the decision is made naively by people who focus on finance, you could end up with a system that's not right for you. Or, you might buy into the hype and miss out on a system that actually handles your core business.

The consequences of these mistakes can be significant. You might end up with a system that doesn't support your business's growth, requiring additional investments to switch systems later. This can cause operational disruptions and increased costs. Furthermore, failing to leverage advanced capabilities like AI due to an inadequate foundation can mean missed opportunities for efficiency and optimisation.

Understanding your needs is like buying a car. Imagine a young couple looking for a new car; a small car works perfectly fine for getting to and from work. It makes sense to buy a small car. However, in the next couple of years, this couple plans to get married and have kids. This means that within the seven years they're likely to be paying off the car, they'll need a family vehicle. If they opt for the small car without the foresight, they'll need to replace it sooner.

In summary, to truly understand your needs and make an informed ERP selection, follow these steps:

- ◆ Identify all high-level business processes across your business.
- ◆ Document the critical touchpoints where data is collected and decisions are made.

- Engage with different departments to gather input on their pain points and future needs.
- Consider your business's future, specifically where you want to be in five to ten years. Ask your team: 'When the new ERP fixes all today's issues, what will we need next and why?'

By taking these steps, you'll ensure your product selection is future-focused and aligned with your long-term strategy. This means your ERP will not only solve your current issues but also support your future growth and evolving needs.

If you are concerned about your ability to do this well, or about the potential self-serving bias of salespeople who offer to help, an independent consultant can guide the process and provide an objective assessment. Either way, by taking these steps, you'll be in a better position to choose a solution that grows with you and truly supports your business goals.

For more tools and templates to help you clearly define your ERP needs, visit **www.shanewilliams.com.au/clusterpuck** and get started on the right path.

# Misunderstanding the ERP cost model

IN 2023, I was contacted by the CEO of a well-established, family-owned Australian company with decades of experience in designing and manufacturing high-quality commercial kitchen equipment.

A couple of years prior, they had embarked on implementing an ERP solution, and their experience was less than ideal. They believed that many of their operational business problems would be solved by the ERP. However, twelve months after the implementation, they found that many of their business needs weren't being met, and they were getting absolutely no support from the partner who had done the implementation.

After a few conversations with the software vendor, the implementation partner, and the client, it became apparent that there was a fundamental disconnect between the client's understanding of what they were paying for and the vendor's understanding of what they were providing. The client assumed that support would be included in the ongoing license costs, while the vendor expected to charge separately for any support services. Additionally, the client didn't realise that the professional services only covered the initial implementation and not the continuous improvements they needed.

ERP solutions effectively have three types of costs within the cost model:

- Professional Services
- Software Licenses
- Support

## Professional Services

The first type of cost in an ERP is professional services. This is typically done under a scope of work and accounts for the people's time to either implement the solution initially or to do incremental improvements to the solution over time. These services are generally billed as time and materials and are provided as needed rather than perpetual. You would expect to use these time-based services for implementation, upgrades and bespoke project work.

## Software Licenses

The second type is the cost of the licenses. These might be a standard price per user, regardless of what functions you use in the tool, or they might be based per module or per capability of the platform. Either way, they are the keys to the kingdom. Each person needs a particular type of license to do their job, and those are generally billed annually in advance for the lifetime of using the solution. You will typically be able to increase your license count as-needs, but cancelling licenses can be problematic.

### Support

The third type of cost is support services. These vary between providers, but the common approaches are typically a fixed fee to secure a fixed amount of hours per month or, in some cases, a cost equal to a percentage of the total license value. It covers the ability of your team to contact somebody in case of need. If the system is not working or your team doesn't understand how something is supposed to work, this support services contract means that you have someone to call. If the problem is serious, the services provider can speak directly to the ERP software vendor and figure out what the problem is. It's these support costs that often get overlooked or misunderstood by customers. The assumption is that since they have paid to implement the software and are paying for licenses, they should just get support. It's a fair assumption, but not how it works. The separation exists to enable the software vendor to bill you for the licenses, but the support vendor to bill you separately for support.

In the case of our friends with the commercial kitchen company, the business case for paying for the support services hadn't been made clear to them. Because they already had a contract saying they were paying monthly for using the software, they couldn't understand why they were being asked to pay more every time they called for support. While arguably it was the responsibility of the implementation partner to describe how the ongoing support services worked, the message hadn't landed. The customer felt that they were being ripped off. They'd already paid for a solution that wasn't working as they needed and weren't prepared to pay any more because they didn't feel like they were getting value out of what they had already paid for. So, they ended up in a stalemate.

The solution to this is fairly simple. Appreciate that there are three types of costs in any ERP and budget for them. Support services are essential to ensure that you get ongoing value from the solution, but they also represent an ongoing cost.

I find the best way to really get your head around this and make sure you're not being stitched up is to look at what you're being asked to pay and consider if you think it's a reasonable cost. If it seems too cheap or too expensive, ask some questions. Not sure if it's reasonable? Fair enough – consider this. If your licenses are worth $120 000 a year and you're quoted an additional 9% to cover support, you're only paying $10 800 for support annually. This doesn't translate to many support hours, especially when the supplier wants to make a margin on their people's time. So what do you think you're likely to get for $10,800 a year? **Red flag.**

Make sure you understand how this particular supplier's support costs work.

If you're buying a guaranteed number of hours per month,

are there any restrictions on how they can be used? Do the hours carry over every month or are they forfeited? If they carry over and you've banked enough of them, can you use them for staff training?

Alternatively, if it's a percentage of the license cost, consider the following:

- How does the support work?
- Does the contract only cover the first X minutes of each call before you have to pay more, or is it some other arrangement?
- Will they help you with 'How do I?' training questions or only break-fix?
- Is there a capped number of calls?
- Is it just someone to answer the phone and log your issue in their system to pass on or do they fix things?
- Will you have to pay extra to have someone investigate and fix the problem?
- What will that cost?

If the answers to these questions don't provide a workable support contract, I'd be looking to negotiate something more realistic before signing up... or looking for another partner.

# Underbaked or overbaked requirements

ANOTHER COMMON MISTAKE SMEs make when implementing new systems is underbaking or overbaking requirements. You often hear about the importance of clear requirements for a successful project. Terms like 'user requirements' and 'functional requirements' are frequently mentioned. However, it's crucial to strike the right balance, and not get caught in the ways many businesses trip up.

A common pitfall is getting trapped in **analysis paralysis**. This happens when businesses spend excessive time intricately documenting every current business process. The rationale is that clearly articulating your current processes will help the implementation team ensure the system works as needed. However, the way you do things has largely been built up over time, accounting for current software solution constraints, and the fluid nature of processes in a growing business. This means the business processes you have in place often aren't optimal and won't serve you in the future. The way you do things isn't necessarily offering you any competitive advantage in your market. Importantly, when your goal is to significantly transform your business, documenting current processes is of little value if those processes won't serve your future needs. Therefore, heavily documenting your current way of working is superfluous, time-consuming and expensive, and the documentation usually becomes outdated quickly.

On the other end of the spectrum, some businesses don't understand their operations well and assume that some sort of Nostradamus or mind reader from the implementation partner's team will magically predict their needs without any visibility into how the business works. How do think that one plays out? If you can't articulate what you do, or at least why you do it, and you can't explain the process in terms of inputs and outputs, then what hope does anyone outside the business have of getting the right outcome? For example, 9 out of 10 businesses implementing an ERP tell me their biggest challenge is operational reporting. Let's say you sell products based on product groups; if these groups aren't correctly defined from the start, the reports generated won't be useful. So, unless you can clearly articulate what you need in terms of insights from your ERP, you can expect that you won't get them. The software folks are essentially skilled trades with years of experience and a van full of the latest tools. Amazing value when you know what you want them to do, but too expensive to have farting around making it up as they go.

Both extremes - too much irrelevant documentation or

simply not enough - lead to the same problem: your requirements are either overbaked or underbaked. and your end result will suffer.

Over-documenting can lead to a project that never starts, or worse, building a bastardised clunky system, while under-documenting can result in a system that doesn't come close to meeting the business's needs. In both cases, you will find yourself back at square one, needing to re-evaluate and re-implement the system, which leads to additional costs and delays.

How do you get this right? Firstly, don't assume your implementation partners are mind readers - you need to articulate your needs in terms of inputs, outputs, and desired results. When doing this, focus on the outcomes you want to achieve, not the small details of how things are done today. Clearly define the key functionalities and insights that will propel your business forward and be open to rethinking your processes and adopting industry best practices offered by the new system.

A practical way to ensure you're striking the right balance is by having your vendor respond to your requirements list in writing, using standard responses such as:

a) 'out of the box,'
b) 'some modification,'
c) 'we have to create that report,'
d) 'we have to create the whole business process.'

Invite them to provide commentary alongside each response.

This structured feedback will help you understand what the system can deliver immediately and what will need more work. Furthermore, these responses will become critical when it comes time to evaluate the prototype - something we'll dive into later.

# Trying to do too much at one time

WITH THE PROSPECT of a new system on the horizon, it's not unusual for folks to get excited. After all, there's the promise of saving on operational costs, improving processes, keeping staff happy, finding new revenue streams, and gaining better visibility into the business for improved forecasting. The problem is, when organisations get over excited and want to get the maximum value from their investment as quickly as possible, they make the mistake of trying to do too many things at once. Some vendors will exacerbate this urgency to sell more licenses, creating manufactured discounts and using pressure tactics like, 'If you sign by this date, I can get you this deal.' These incentives encourage businesses to commit to more than they can realistically implement at one time.

This approach is problematic for a number of reasons. Licensing incentives, such as free licenses or license holiday incentives, convert to paid licenses before you even go live with the first phase. Any discounts you receive for purchasing 'future needs' modules up front are soon eroded - it's common for businesses to pay for system capabilities for years before being ready to leverage them.

What you want is a phased approach to your ERP adoption.

As emphasised in 'Enterprise Resource Planning Systems: Systems, Life Cycle, Electronic Commerce, and Risk' by Daniel E. O'Leary, implementing the ERP system in stages helps mitigate risks by allowing early identification and resolution of issues, thus reducing the likelihood of major disruptions. You need to build all the foundational capabilities, migrate your data, test, train your people, and manage a successful go-live well before you have any chance of using the additional capabilities.

The consequences of overcommitting are significant. Paying for licenses and modules that you can't use for a long time prevents you from achieving the return you expected from your investment. Not only that, but stretching your team creates distraction and prevents focus on what is most important: building a solid foundation. By focusing on core functionalities first, as O'Leary suggests, businesses ensure that essential operations are running smoothly before adding more complex features.

One of my previous clients, a family-owned business based in regional NSW that manufactures and installs industrial water pumps, had completed a sales process with an ERP vendor. The ERP sales team pressured them into signing a contract before Christmas to get an 'end-of-year' discount. The deal was 17 months, including five months free. What a bargain! The business owner signed the contract in good faith, eager to leverage the discount and get the contract off his to-do list before the Christmas holidays. But the reality was that they weren't ready to kick off their project for several months. They wouldn't even start their project until May and wouldn't be ready to go live until close to December. This meant that the so-called free licenses had already converted to paid licenses before they even started their project kickoff. Seven months later, when they were ready to go live, they had already paid for seven months worth of licenses – not only for the core product, but also for additional modules they wouldn't be ready to use for at least a further 12 months.

The lesson is clear: the only way to eat an elephant is one bite at a time.

First, focus on building core foundational capabilities and targeting low-hanging fruit: the high-impact, low-effort processes that build capability and provide immediate ROI. You'll likely already know what those are. Where does your team do manual things they shouldn't need to? Perhaps look at automating invoicing, barcoding inventory, or moving to digital time sheets to remove hours of manual effort and mistakes from re-keying off paper forms. Stick to getting the basics right and focus on the harder stuff later.

Second, most up-front software discounts are just traps to get you to buy things you don't necessarily need or before you really need them. They're the shit garlic bread you're going to throw out because the pizza is enough. It's simply a trap for young players; you don't need those extras now, and they won't save you money in the long run. The best approach is to ignore the sales tactics and purchase the bare minimum licenses needed for the core modules and only enough to set up and configure the system. As noted by O'Leary, this phased approach breaks down the implementation into manageable parts, reducing complexity and allowing the team to concentrate on specific areas. When you're almost ready to go live and need to bring people into the system for testing, then buy the additional licenses for those folks. Later, when you're ready to take on additional capabilities, consider purchasing the additional module licenses. There is almost always no benefit to signing up for the licenses upfront. You won't be able to go as fast or build as much as you think you can on day one.

# PART 1A

# VENDOR SELECTION

# Chasing shiny things or hollow promises

DURING AN ERP sales pitch, software vendors are always looking to gain a competitive edge, often using differentiation as a tactic to persuade you to choose their product over another.

When evaluating their options, folks often get swayed by flashy features and buzzwords like AI, blockchain, and Big Data. These terms sound impressive and might seem useful after a salesperson's explanation, but the reality is that you often need a robust platform with well-implemented processes and clean data before these features can be beneficial.

The problem with chasing shiny things is that great marketing does not equal a great product or a fit-for-purpose product. A fit-for-purpose product is one that meets your needs now *and* in the future, and is priced relative to your investment profile. When you get swayed by shiny features, you risk investing in a product that doesn't truly meet your core requirements, potentially leading to wasted resources and unmet expectations.

Another mistake that I often see is the reliance on hollow

promises. These promises often manifest during the sales process when vendors identify critical requirements they can't deliver on. They then make promises about future features to solve those problems. A common line is, 'I've spoken to the product team, and that particular feature is in the next release.' This statement is almost always bullshit – especially if it doesn't get recorded in the contract. In my decades of experience, I've seen countless vendors make such promises, only to disappoint later. If you ever attend a large software industry trade show, you'll notice all the software vendors start their presentations with a 'Safe Harbour statement', a legal disclaimer indicating that future capabilities they discuss might never material- ise. Despite the hype, nothing is guaranteed until it's actu- ally delivered.

A few years ago, I worked with a family-owned business with 50 employees, specialising in custom-engineered infra- structure solutions for coastal protection and sustainability. They manufacture components like steel supports for piers and control modules for floodgates, which are installed by their team of engineers and construction specialists. On the verge of picking up big government infrastructure projects, the leader- ship team were looking for an ERP that included better tools to manage their projects and costing. This business developed a detailed, costed project plan as part of a tender response rather than a standard practice of building a project plan upon being awarded the contract. They believed this process ensured their quotes came in on budget and allowed them to move projects straight into action when they won the business.

During their ERP search, nothing out of the box allowed them to build an entire project plan at the beginning of the process. However, a vendor promised that, if they inked a deal, this capability would be prioritised in the next release, set to be completed in eight weeks. Based on this promise, the business bought the software. Almost two years later, the feature hadn't arrived. They continued using their old Google Sheets process to build project plans, keying the data into the ERP later. They invested tens of thousands of dollars for limited benefit, based on a broken promise from the salespeople. There was no contractual obligation to deliver the promised feature.

The other type of hollow promise is providing something of value as an incentive to sign up. For example, 'If you sign the deal this month, I can get you included on our customer appreciation trip to the Melbourne Cup,' or, 'We've got a six-month lead time on our project resources, but I've had a word with the delivery director, and if you to sign this contract today, he's going to slot you in so we can hit your timeline.'

To this point, my favourite story involves a client looking at contracting solutions for a highly successful Melbourne-based business with a workforce 1500 strong. The sales rep offered a 10% discount and free implementation. Alarm bells went off immediately: new product, no existing clients, and promises of free implementation but no mention of it on the contract.

Despite my strong counsel against it, the client signed the deal. 'I'll make them honour it,' he quipped.

Immediately upon signing the contract, reality hit. The promise of 'free implementation' had been a misunderstanding. The salesperson had 'misinterpreted' a message from the US practice director, who had agreed to make an expert available to assist with the implementation - but not to waive the fee entirely. The phrase, 'We'll make someone free for the implementation,' was never meant to mean free of charge. A convenient mistake? We'll never know. What's certain is that the client ended up with an unproven product and an expensive implementation, a classic reminder that if something seems too good to be true, it probably is. And while it's not my style to say 'I told you so', Norm, if you're reading this, **I fucking told you so**.

In summary, chasing shiny things and believing in hollow promises can lead to wasted resources, unmet expectations, and significant operational inefficiencies. The advice here is straightforward:

- ◆ Don't buy anything based on promises of future features. Buy what's generally available and what you can see in a real customer environment.
- ◆ Don't fall for a high-pressure sale tied to a deadline on the promise of a future incentive.
- ◆ If it's not written in the contract, assume it doesn't exist.

# MISTAKE 6

# Buying the sales team and not the delivery team

THIS MISTAKE SEEMS ridiculously obvious when we talk about it, yet more often than not, people just don't consider it when they're in the moment. Unfortunately, although it's all too common, it can have drastic ramifications for the success of your project.

In the early part of an engagement with a software implementation organisation, you will meet a team consisting of salespeople and pre-sales engineers. Their goal is to understand enough about your business to showcase how their solution could work for you. They address your specific requirements and give you a flavour of how they will solve those issues to instil confidence in you to purchase the solution. Remember, their strong suit is painting their product in its best light, allaying your concerns, and giving you a sense of confidence to make a purchase.

The problem arises because this team doesn't implement the system. Realistically, from an implementation partner, that's what you're buying. If you're buying implementation and ongoing support, who do you really need confidence in? It's the **delivery team.**

Failing to recognise this can lead to significant issues. It's like talking to a designer and a land sales agent versus talking to the builder. The first two can paint a good picture and provide you with a cost estimate, but the builder is your key to success. Do they do good work? Can you work with them? Are they familiar with the area and understand the rock content of the land you're intending to purchase? At the end of the day, the designer and the land salespeople are knowledgeable and probably well-intentioned, but their job is to get you to buy. The builder is the person who's going to do the work. It's pointless to agree to have a house built and then have a builder show up on site and tell you, 'Oh, by the way, we need to blast this block, and it just added $100 000 to your invoice.' Or to find out that the builder they propose to use is actually your ex-wife's husband and you just aren't going to get along.

Consider the plight of a regional NSW manufacturer of agricultural equipment. Looking to expand into international markets, they undertook a rigorous ERP selection process. They selected the solution after the sales team gave them complete confidence in the solution (and more than a couple of long lunches). After signing the contract, the project was handed over to the delivery team, who were offshore, in a different time zone, spoke limited English, and many of whom had only recently joined the organisation so had little to no experience with the ERP product or manufacturing in general. Twelve months after the project kickoff, the solution was still not implemented due to a comedy of errors and a lack of capability in the delivery team. The sales guys stopped answering calls. Meanwhile, the business had paid for the implementation services upfront and had by now paid for several months of licenses they couldn't use. The delay also inhibited their international expansion plans.

The only answer to this problem is to insist on meeting the delivery team prior to signing the agreement. Many of these consultancies have a bench of people who get put onto different projects at different times, so you won't necessarily meet everybody who's going to be on your project. That will depend on the availability of both you and the people within their organisation. But you can certainly get a sense of the types of people they have, and you should absolutely demand to meet the person responsible for making sure your project gets delivered, such as the practice lead or delivery director. You want to know a name, a face, an email address, and a phone number. You want to eyeball them and gain confidence in their ability to work with you to ensure you get the best outcome. Only once you have confidence in that relationship and have had the chance to meet two or three of the types of people you would be working with should you commit to purchasing anything.

# Failing to talk to existing customers

IN THE 2020s, does anyone go to a restaurant without first looking at some sort of online review? What about scrolling through eBay or Amazon for the ideal gift for your other half? The answer is no. Everyone uses ratings and reviews to help them make purchasing decisions.

Yet, when it comes to software implementations, some people make the mistake of bypassing these simple checks. Over a charity game of golf, they come across the beer cart sponsored by a particular solution provider. So, they reach out to the software vendor, get a quote, and just sign it. Or maybe they independently look at a few websites and ask for a demo; then the salespeople do such a great job convincing them that they're great partners, they believe they don't need to talk to anyone else.

Maybe one of the lads at the footy club uses a particular solution. But your buddy's business is not like yours – he works in a CBD consultancy firm, not smashing out hundreds of shower frames a week. His problems are not the same as yours. The people who work for you are not the same as those who work for him. And there's no guarantee that the people who implemented the software for him will be the ones doing it for you.

A common argument I hear is that there's limited value in talking to existing customers because vendors won't put you in front of unhappy customers. So by definition, all you'll hear is that the product is great, and therefore, there is no value in the conversation. But I disagree. In my experience, regardless of who you're put in front of, most people are genuine. They will tell you what works, what doesn't, the challenges they have faced, and what to look out for. For example, you might love your new motorbike and recommend it to anyone, but you also wish the handlebars were a little higher, the seat a little lower, or it had more top-end power. It doesn't mean you're dissatisfied – you're still recommending it – it just means that it's not perfect. When you share that information with your friends, you might find that ride height is super important to them because they're a foot shorter than you. The same applies in the software world. Regardless of whether you're talking to happy customers, most people will still tell you everything you ask, warts and all.

Ignoring this step can lead to significant issues down the line. If you don't understand the strengths *and* limitations of the software from people who are using it in a similar context to yours, you might end up with a solution that doesn't fully meet your needs. This can result in wasted time, additional costs for modifications, or even having to switch to a different solution altogether, causing further disruption to your business.

To illustrate the value of these discussions, let me share a short story. In 2023, I was helping a Melbourne-based horticultural business determine the best ERP solution for their growing business. For several months, the vendor struggled to find a suitable reference because they couldn't find a horticultural business that had used the preferred ERP and wasn't a direct competitor. They ended up with a couple of references, one of which was a local logistics company. The member of the finance team who responded to the reference call was complimentary of the solution and explained their selection and implementation process. She gave background on her company and, through the conversation, drew parallels between the organisations. This allowed for a deeper conversation around the capabilities of the solution, what worked well, what didn't, and how they resolved the problems. She also shared what support looked like after implementation.

Interestingly, what came out of the discussion was that one of the plugins to the ERP being suggested by the implementation partner had been tried and abandoned by this customer. Based on this conversation, the horticultural business was able to go back to the implementation partner and challenge the use of this particular plugin. Ultimately, a different product was selected. That's not to suggest that the initial product wouldn't have worked. But with a greater understanding of what the tool was supposed to do and a deeper dive into its applicability, it created the opportunity for reassessment and adjustment to the plan before a single contract had been signed or a dollar spent.

The basic rule of thumb is if the partner can't provide both types of references – those that verify the software's suitability for your business and those that vouch for the implementation partner's effectiveness – it's a red flag. You should spend ample time talking to existing customers.

The questions you want answered are:

- What are the shortcomings of the product and how did the other customer get past them?
- What do they like about the tool?
- How is their relationship with their implementation partner?
- How well does the partner understand your industry?
- What advice do they have on getting the best value from them?
- What does support look like after implementation?
- Are there any 'gotchas' in the contract you might want to consider?
- What would they have done differently?

These questions will help you understand both the strengths and limitations of the software and the effectiveness of the implementation partner from people who are using it in a similar context to yours. Importantly, even if the lessons are not directly relevant because you're a different business, they often still apply.

In summary, just as you would not make personal purchasing decisions without consulting reviews, the same diligence should apply to software implementations. Talk to existing customers in your industry and those using the same software to understand both the benefits and the limitations. This thorough vetting process can save you from costly mistakes and ensure that the solution you choose truly meets your business needs.

# Becoming unwittingly caught in a multivendor standoff

BUSINESSES BUYING ERP software can sometimes find themselves in an inadvertent Mexican standoff. This occurs when an ERP solution broadly covers most, but not all, of the capabilities you need. Some of your requirements may be more specific or require a depth of capability beyond their out-of-the-box offering.

When the sales folks demonstrate the solution, it appears to be a comprehensive response to your requirements, showing that their product can deliver everything. However, what is actually happening is the creation of an architecture of several integrated systems.

Because most Manufacturing ERP buyers are not technical folks, they wouldn't necessarily realise they're buying a complex integrated software solution. This approach is not necessarily bad so long as you go in with your eyes wide open. The problem arises after implementation. If something goes wrong or the system isn't working as expected and you call for support, the provider may claim they only support their ERP, not the other solutions. You end up stuck in the middle, having to call a third party you've never corresponded with about a software solution you're using. The third party may claim their software is working fine, shifting the blame back to the ERP vendor. You're left stuck in the middle of two vendors shifting blame, and no ability to resolve the problem yourself.

I recently met with a company that does precision manufacturing for the aerospace industry. They have about 90 staff and a $120 million turnover. When they were looking for an ERP solution, it was really important to them to be able to calculate activity-based costing. Their fabricators' hands can get quite dirty, and with the previous system, the staff had struggled with fingerprint technology for their activity tracking. The new solution provided as part of the ERP implementation included facial recognition — a vast improvement. The system worked fine until they got a new employee who was onboarded through the HR process in the new ERP system, but they didn't appear in the timekeeping software. The supervisor called for support, only to be told that the ERP was working fine and they needed to call the third-party vendor themselves. Although they recognised the name from the software application on the iPad recording the facial recognition, they'd never even considered that this was a third-party product with independent support. They didn't have any contact details for these people, had never spoken to them, and it took several weeks to get the new recruit live while the office admin managed the juggling of the support calls between the two vendors.

To avoid this situation, you can explicitly ask the following questions about the bill of materials in the proposal:

- Which products are out-of-the-box capabilities of the ERP they recommend?
- Which line items are third-party products?
- Who will implement and support the integration of those products?
- Once the system is live, who will be responsible for support?
- Will there be one or two software & support contracts?

You're looking for a situation where you have only one support process to manage. If there are third-party products involved, it is the responsibility of the vendors to negotiate amongst themselves regarding ticket logging, escalation and resolution management.

Ideally, when you contract for a multi-product solution, you want a single implementation and support partner upon whom you can rely on owning the implementation and ongoing support.

# PART 1B

# PRODUCT SELECTION

# Buying an unproven product

IT'S GENERALLY NOT a good idea to adopt an unproven or new product, or a solution from overseas that has no local support. It can be very tempting, especially when vendors promise substantial savings and cutting-edge technology. However, this approach is fraught with risk and rarely plays out well. Unless you have a high-risk appetite or a unique business for which there is no local solution, you should steer clear. In this chapter, we'll explore two angles: first, the challenges of adopting overseas software that requires extensive localization and lacks local support; and second, the risks of committing to software that doesn't yet exist but is promised to be built. Let's delve into why these situations often lead to trouble.

Committing to co-developing the localisation of an overseas vendor's product requires significant effort. Suppliers must adapt their software to a new market, considering factors like legislation, taxation, and other unique requirements. The amount of localisation needed for a software vendor to gain market share in a new environment quickly becomes apparent. Even if the overseas vendor says, 'We don't have a footprint in this market or local support, but we'll make you our anchor client and invest in the solution at no cost to you,' many examples show this often doesn't play out well for the client, despite assurances.

For example, what if halfway through the implementation, after you've invested significant time and money, they give up? They might say, 'We didn't realise how complex your local market was and we don't think it's worth the investment right now,' and then pull out. What if they believe they've made enough changes for it to work for you, but when you go live, it doesn't meet your expectations? How will you fix the problem? Will the cost fall on you or them? How much time and effort are you willing to spend helping them build their business while yours suffers?

In 2020, an Australian logistics business with operations in every mainland state and a fleet of several hundred prime movers, sought an ERP solution to enhance operations. A UK-based technology company, offering a suite of purpose-built products for various industries including logistics, responded to the tender. This international group presented a compelling case, leveraging their solutions that were successful in large-scale businesses across North America and Europe. They committed to flying experts to Australia to work directly with the customer to build the necessary localisation and share the costs. However, the challenges in localising the product and adapting it to satisfy local unions and state transport regulations were significant. After twelve months, several hundred thousand dollars of investment, and two failed go-live attempts, the CEO abandoned the project. Not only had they lost their investment of time and money, but the international vendor indicated an intent to sue them for the value of their investment and potential lost earnings in the Australian market.

A second area of concern is purchasing 'vapourware' – software that either doesn't exist or lacks promised capabilities, with vendors claiming these features will come in 'the next release'. The trap is that these vendors might claim they have an industry-specific solution to get you to commit to buying it. In reality, they often intend to create the product only once they have a buyer. The risk is that you invest your money before realising they don't actually have a solution. You end up paying them to develop a product, which takes significantly longer than buying something off the shelf that already works. Worse, all that investment goes straight into their IP, allowing them to resell the solution you've paid to develop.

A classic example is the hundred-million-dollar lawsuit filed by Waste Management USA against SAP. Waste Management claimed that SAP had promised 'a waste industry standard solution with no customisation required.' In reality, no such solution existed. SAP had mocked-up a demo to sell the product with the intention of building it on Waste Management's dime. Not only did they buy something that didn't exist, but the lawsuit suggested that SAP couldn't deliver after the fact.

A further risk is that even when a solution already exists, adopting an overseas product with no local support can be problematic. Although the vendor may send people to help with implementation, they're unlikely to set up local support unless they've done so via partnership beforehand. Many international vendors will commit to 24-hour support, but in reality, their team is not in your time zone. Consider this: unless you are running a 24-hour operation, there's a good chance that your own key people don't work overnight. Why assume that the software vendor's most experienced people will be awake during your critical business hours? What level of support can you genuinely expect when their key people are asleep? Often, 24-hour support means someone will answer the phone or an email and acknowledge your issue. Depending on the severity, determined by the person answering the phone, they might not wake someone up. You may not get help until their next working day, causing significant downtime for your business.

Some international solution providers, in the early stages of entering a new market, may partner with local suppliers to handle localisation and support. This is a step better than having no local support, but it often means the majority of customisation costs fall on you. You may also become the guinea pig as they iron out the kinks. Using an international product without local support usually benefits the vendor, not you. The commercials often don't make sense when you consider the problem holistically.

The only time you should consider this high-risk approach

is if you operate in a very niche industry that can't be serviced locally. For instance, one of my clients is a global leader in vertical farming, specifically in the germination of seedlings. Their unique business model means there are no locally developed or supported software solutions for their niche. The CEO feels they have no option but to invest in an international product. This approach is fraught with risk, and unless you absolutely must do it, I would advise against it. But, if you have to, my advice is to consider the ongoing support arrangement before signing a contract. Ideally, get them to engage with a local implementation partner, train and support this local provider, and have the implementation and support done by the local company. This ensures you have someone in your time zone, who understands your implementation, and can provide local support. As a bonus, an implementation partner has a better chance of getting support from the international vendor than you will because the software company sees the local partner as a gateway to more customers.

To ensure you're asking the right questions about product localisation and support, visit **www.shanewilliams.com.au/ clusterpuck** for more resources.

MISTAKE
10

# Selecting a product with limited service providers

WHEN IT COMES to choosing an ERP system, the number of service providers often doesn't come to mind — but it should. Opinions amongst my peers differ on how much this matters, but I'm convinced that overlooking this factor will lead to significant challenges down the line.

Essentially, there are two types of ERP products: those with a **closed ecosystem** and those with an **open** one. In a closed ecosystem, the supplier of the software is also the sole supplier of services, controlling everything from the software to the support. Some of my peers argue that this is an advantage because a single provider gives you one throat to choke. When things are working well you have a single point of contact for software and services; and when things go wrong, there's no ability for people to point fingers in a different direction.

In contrast, an open ecosystem is where the software vendor either doesn't supply services at all, relying entirely on third parties, or provides services alongside certified implementation partners.

In my view, it's a mistake to pick the single-vendor closed ecosystem unless you have very unique circumstances. Here's why.

Having only one supplier limits your flexibility to choose who implements and supports your system. Flexibility offers several benefits. For one, a lack of competitive pressure gives you no leverage over what you are charged for your implementation project. You'll pay what you're told – and if the project cost blows out, you have nowhere to turn.

With vendor independence, you can switch suppliers if you're not satisfied with the quality or cost of post-implementation support. Competition means there's pressure to remain cost-competitive and maintain high standards in service and support. Although it takes time for a new vendor to get up to speed on your system configuration, it means that if your relationship with your current supplier sours, you have options.

Conversely, if there is only one provider of services and you encounter a worst-case scenario, your only option may be to switch systems entirely. This is a hugely expensive and disruptive exercise. But when subpar service becomes so disruptive that your business is at risk, you won't have a choice.

A custom furniture manufacturer based in Perth, with annual revenue of around $50 million and a workforce of 75 staff, specialises in bespoke furniture pieces for high-end clients. Experiencing 20% year-over-year growth, the company sought to upgrade to an ERP system that could seamlessly manage e-commerce, custom orders, inventory, and production schedules. Unfortunately, they learned the lesson the hard way when their chosen system failed to meet their needs.

The company selected a bespoke custom manufacturing ERP solution from a single vendor, influenced by the vendor's promises of industry experience, seamless integration, and comprehensive support. Initially, the implementation phase appeared promising. However, as the project progressed, several gaps in the system's capabilities emerged. Critical functionalities, such as custom order processing and e-commerce integration, required extensive customisations. These necessary adjustments significantly increased the project's cost, but the company continued, believing these changes would eventually lead to improved efficiency and productivity.

After going live, the company faced significant challenges. During the first major system upgrade, the company discovered their customisations were incompatible with the new ERP version. The vendor claimed the original developer of the customisations was no longer with the business, and the remaining staff were unwilling to troubleshoot the developer's code. The solution proposed was to redevelop the customisations from scratch, at a substantial cost.

With no flexibility to find another developer, the company had no choice but to comply. The company has had to invest significant amounts to re-customise the ERP system after each upgrade. The lack of competitive pressure means the vendor had little incentive to improve service quality or offer reasonable pricing.

This experience highlighted the critical risks of relying on a single-vendor closed ecosystem for ERP solutions.

In my opinion, selecting a product with a diversified range of implementation partners should be the default. You should only consider a single-provider solution after a thorough critical analysis of your needs and use case. If the uniqueness of your business, market, or industry justifies the risk of single-vendor lock-in, then so be it. If that's the case, before signing a contract, go to the market to find people in your local area who have experience implementing, configuring, and using the tool. Effectively self-insure your business against the risk. While an independent contractor isn't as ideal as a list of certified partners, it at least offers some independent advice and support to help you assess the configuration changes necessary to adapt the solution as your business evolves.

MISTAKE
11

# Clinging to on-premise solutions in a cloud-based world

MANY BUSINESS OWNERS think of an ERP system like they would a piece of manufacturing equipment – something physical and tangible that you can see and touch. But modern technology solutions look nothing like your typical manufacturing investment in terms of where they run, how you access them and how you pay for them.

This mistake manifests because most manufacturing leaders are used to the traditional way of purchasing technology: pay money for a tangible asset that sits in your facility; something material that you can look at. Typically, in manufacturing, that's a piece of machinery or a robot. As far as an ERP goes, they believe that if they have a server sitting in the cupboard somewhere that they can go and look at and touch, then they're actually getting something material for their money.

But the industry has moved on since the 1990s when cloud

solutions didn't exist, and the software model was very much a capital purchase where you owned the licenses in perpetuity and depreciated them over time. In the 2020s, most ERP software licensing, whether on-premise or cloud, is structured as an opex cost – effectively a lease – and most vendors are offering or recommending that they host the solution for you. This new model has benefits that a lot of growing manufacturing business owners may not appreciate.

The belief in owning physical assets can lead businesses to overlook the flexibility and efficiency that cloud solutions offer. In today's fast-paced world, being stuck managing on-premise IT hardware and software can be a significant disadvantage. Managing computer rooms, air conditioning, power supply, backup and restore software, and patching: all these are necessary requirements for maintaining robust on-premise ERP solutions, but they're nuisances you no longer need to deal with.

To illustrate, think about the difference between a subscription to Spotify versus owning your CDs. The CDs were great because they gave you the sense of making a one-time purchase and that you owned something physical. But really, the reason for buying them was that there was no other way. What you really wanted was the experience of listening to the music. Now, in the 2020s, while you still want to listen to music, most folks don't have any desire to be stuck managing CD player equipment, struggling with scratched and missing CDs, or managing fights between family members over whose turn it is to listen. You're happy to just pay for the subscription and know that everybody can listen to what they want when they want, simultaneously or not, and that somebody else is taking care of all the nonsense that is not listening to music.

A significant factor to consider is cybersecurity. The exponentially growing threat of cyber criminals makes managing on-premise solutions risky. Even if you have a solid internal IT team, studies have shown that cloud service providers 'handle data security and compliance with specialised teams, often exceeding what individual businesses can achieve'. By leveraging the expertise of cloud service providers, you can mitigate risks and focus on your core business operations without the constant worry of cyber threats.

As technology and our workforce changes, clinging to on-premise solutions makes less sense.

I was recently introduced to a family-owned business who manufacture specialised equipment for the healthcare sector. As the business grew, they sold in facilities across the country increasing the need for reliable remote access to the ERP.

A couple of years ago, they upgraded their ERP but chose to stay with an on-premise solution. Despite having a modern IT infrastructure, managing the on-premise ERP became challenging. The burden of maintaining a server room, ensuring data security, and handling software updates proved problematic, especially when their internal IT specialist moved on.

In hindsight, the head of operations realised that a cloud-based ERP would have been a better choice. The vendor would manage the infrastructure and security, allowing their IT team to focus on strategic tasks. A cloud-based solution would also ensure seamless access for all employees, regardless of location, and eliminate the need to invest in and maintain physical infrastructure.

My recommendation is to think about what your core capabilities are as a business. Typically, as a manufacturer, you're really good at making things; but unless those things are IT hardware and software, you shouldn't be trying to manage IT hardware and software. So, leave the management and protection of your IT solutions to businesses that specialise in it. This allows you to focus on your core business activities while ensuring your IT infrastructure is secure, reliable and scalable.

# PART 2

IMPLEMENTATION

# Not paying for a detailed scope and prototype

EAGER AND AMBITIOUS but often pressed for time, business leaders can be tempted to rely solely on pre-sales activity as enough evidence that a proposed solution will work for their business. Prematurely signing up for a full implementation is a mistake that can literally cost you thousands. The goal of the sales team is to take a superficial look at the pain points you're telling them about and present a picture of the world where your future experience is amazing. They don't yet have the requisite level of detail to understand how this tool will actually work in your business.

This happens because the pre-sales process is designed to give you confidence in the solution through a polished and appealing presentation. Sales teams aim to highlight how the product can address your business challenges in a broad, optimistic manner. However, they lack the depth of insight into your specific operational nuances and potential integration challenges. As a result, it's easy for business leaders to be swayed by the positive outlook and skip the more rigorous evaluation stages.

The mistake here is bypassing detailed scoping and a prototype phase. Without these steps, you may not uncover crucial issues until after a significant investment has been made. This can lead to unexpected challenges and the realisation that the proposed solution is incomplete, requiring more customisation and configuration than initially anticipated.

The consequences of this mistake can be severe. Once you delve into the details, you're likely to encounter genuine business challenges or additional scope that you hadn't considered. This not only delays the project but also increases costs significantly. Furthermore, the initial promise of value may not be delivered without extensive additional work, which can be frustrating and costly. Your team may also face disruption, training challenges, and change management issues that were not anticipated, impacting overall productivity and morale.

This process is similar to test-driving a car. Some dealers now offer the option to take a car for the entire weekend to see how it fits with your family. It's one thing to see a vehicle on TV, online or in the showroom, but it's another to take it for a test drive. Seeing how it feels and using it in your day-to-day life before determining if it's fit for purpose is invaluable. Imagine buying a car off the showroom floor and being told by the salesperson that you can bring it back in a couple of weeks to have your towbar fitted so you can tow your caravan, only to find out once you're signed up to a five-year lease that the vehicle doesn't have the requisite horsepower. Taking a demo car away for a weekend, attaching the van, and attempting to tow would have highlighted that problem quickly and saved you a bunch of headaches trying to change over the car to something more appropriate.

Dianne Semmens, an ERP implementation expert, offers the following advice for those looking to secure an ERP system. She emphasises the importance of a detailed scope and a paid prototype phase: 'I think the biggest thing is not actually delving into paying for a detailed scope with the software.' Often, software salespeople assure potential customers that the system will handle various tasks, but 'it's only when they actually start trialing the software that they think, 'Oh God, it doesn't do what we thought it would do. It doesn't do this how we do it. It doesn't do what we explained.' To avoid such pitfalls, Semmens recommends conducting a paid prototype phase. She suggests, 'Doing a paid prototype, you know, a little bit more than just a paid scope. Just saying to the software vendor, "Look, we really like and think that you've got the right application for us, but instead of us sinking 100 grand into it, let's just spend five grand on it."' This allows the vendor to demonstrate that the software can perform the essential tasks the business needs, proving that 'it really works before we spend the big picture money'. Semmens adds, 'We just spent 15 hours with someone proving that we can do what we need to do, and now it's like, "Okay, we'll sign up with the software"'.

So, for your peace of mind, make sure you do a prototype.

But don't fall into the trap of accidentally turning the prototype into a 99% complete build. The prototype should provide a detailed set of design documents explaining how your requirements will be met and demonstrate where unique capabilities need configuration or customisation.

Focus your investment on proving how the solution will handle your unique business processes. The vendor should demonstrate basic functions using out-of-the-box capabilities, with no need for significant configuration or loading large amounts of your business data. You should not pay for these standard demonstrations. Instead, your investment should be in areas where the partner's design intends to materially change how the solution works out of the box to suit your business. This targeted approach ensures that only the unique elements of your business processes are tested and validated, providing confidence that the solution will meet your needs, without committing to full implementation costs prematurely. The rule of thumb is that you should aim to spend less than 20% of your total services budget to get to the end of the prototype stage.

It's important to note that this is not wasted money. The value of detailed scoping is that after seeing the prototype, you will have a clear understanding of your future costs, expectations and preparation for estimated delivery time and change management with much greater certainty. Assuming you are going ahead with the build, this is money you would have spent anyway. You're simply creating a clear decision gate in the project to allow everyone to reflect and have far more certainty about what you're going to get and what it's going to cost. It's also a great opportunity to try on not only the software but also, equally as important, the implementation team.

## MISTAKE 13

# Customisation

I HONESTLY CONSIDERED having a chapter with only two words:

**'Just Don't.'**

But in all honesty, 'customisation' is a bit more nuanced than that.

I reckon you'll agree that every business is different, and so by extension, no product designed for many businesses will be a perfect fit for any single business. Having said that, I stand by the rule that the cheapest, easiest and best way to implement any new ERP software is by adopting most of the processes as they are designed in the solution out of the box.

'But we found the perfect ERP?'

No you didn't. Any salesperson that tells you their solution can do everything that you need is full of shit. You might find a product that can handle most of your business processes, but if a vendor claims they've got you 100% covered, chances are customisation is involved.

The reason I said customisation is nuanced is that not all customisations are created equal. There are essentially two types of customisation – configuration and code. What you need to know is the type, cost and complexity of the customisation required to serve your need.

If the customisation can be made without needing a software developer, or if your internal team can learn to adjust the product to meet your needs and continue to manage and improve it, that's configuration. This is manageable. And as a bonus, with configuration, upgrades will generally work without issues.

However, if you need some hardcore programmatic customisation, then you need to rethink the requirement (or the ERP). Code comes with a high price tag and ongoing risks of maintenance and support challenges – so beware!

So, let's say you're comfortable enough with the proposed ERP and anticipated level and type of customisation; how do we put some guardrails on to protect your investment?

During discovery and design, have the vendor discuss how their system is designed to work and, with the involvement of your team, create a detailed set of functional and non-functional specifications. As I said earlier, aim to use the system processes as the vendor intended, because adopting standardisation means you get something easy to build, easy to maintain, and scalable. Yes, it's a change in how you do things, but the way you did them isn't necessarily better than the system's way, and it avoids heavy customisation. The key is to let this process flow, guided by the experts.

The exception to adopting standardised processes is if you have a particular process that genuinely offers a competitive advantage. If, with a critical eye, you believe that the way you do something differentiates you in the market, then document that thoroughly and ensure it's included when the new system is built. For the most part, these unique processes will account for less than 10% of the overall solution, saving you thousands on implementation costs by using the system as designed.

It might help to think about adopting your ERP as if you were buying a new GPS. Imagine that documenting your business processes is a bit like creating directions from your house to your holiday destination. You could spend a lot of time figuring out every single turn and waypoint to get you all the way to your destination, and then programming the entire itinerary into the GPS. It would work, but would also largely negate any value you get from the system. A better way would be to let the product work as the manufacturer intended. If there's a specific waypoint you want the GPS to go through, much like a unique process in your business that you want to maintain, you could simply tell the GPS to go through this waypoint and let it handle the rest.

A common pushback I get to adopting new processes is based on the perception that change management will be too significant. If the new system can be made to work like the old one, the thinking goes that it will reduce change management efforts. While I hear the argument, the reality is that, time and time again, the consequences of customisation massively outweigh the short-term benefits.

When thinking about ERP implementations, my advice is to understand where you're headed in terms of your overarching business process flow. Then, focus on ensuring that the specific waypoints, or critical processes that provide a competitive advantage, are included, and let the system optimise the rest of the route for you.

A Sydney-based business that sources, imports and distributes FMCG specialty products undertook an ERP implementation. The warehouse manager, who was given the responsibility to work with the vendor to implement the warehouse part of the system, decided that his unique process for inventory management was so valuable that the system had to be entirely customised to support it.

Initially, the project was on track, and the system went live successfully. However, shortly after go-live, significant issues emerged in the upstream and downstream parts of the business due to problems with inventory.

The warehouse manager was very set in his ways and insisted on customising the new Warehouse Management module to match the old system. The project manager explained: 'He reverse-engineered this nice new clean system. Literally got them to reprogram it back to the old system he was using. That was just the way he worked.'

The extensive customisations made to accommodate the warehouse manager's unique process created significant impacts on the stock ordering part of the ERP, and created a system that did not leverage the new technology's advantages.

This led to significant operational inefficiencies, as well as over-stocking and stockouts.

The post-implementation review revealed that none of the customisations provided any advantage to the organisation except to appease the warehouse manager. Ironically, he was retiring at the end of the year anyway.

Despite having a fixed price for the implementation, they ended up spending thousands more to remove the customi-sations. And because they had to do these changes while the system was live, it caused a tonne of business interruption.

The project manager reflected, 'We then took like a month to undo some of this stuff and get it back to where it should be.' This situation highlights the risks and costs associated with unnecessary customisations, emphasising the importance of aligning new systems with modern best practices rather than outdated processes.

Learn more about managing customisation effectively by visiting **www.shanewilliams.com.au/clusterpuck** for addi-tional insights and resources.

# Creating complexity that doesn't serve your business

DID YOU EVER see the early seasons of MasterChef? Not the current version, where the contestants have skills suggesting they've been tutored by a Michelin star chef. I mean the early ones where it genuinely felt like the people on the show were average folks like you and me, and that if you had a passion for cooking and some sense of how to get around the kitchen, you might have been able to compete.

I think the journey of a home cook becoming a chef is a great analogy for how technology needs grow and reshape over time.

You start out in your home kitchen watching videos on YouTube, and as you try out new ideas and cooking styles, you start to buy various gadgets. Over time, you have too many gadgets and the kitchen becomes crowded, but your passion continues.

So you open a small café. You could bring your arsenal of

gadgets with you, but the smarter move is to reset, reduce complexity, and make sure you have the right equipment to provide a good customer experience without overcapitalising. So you end up buying some versatile appliances that give you additional capabilities without taking up too much space in your small café kitchen.

Investing in technology in your business follows a similar life cycle. You start out small, probably with just a small business finance system and email. As the business grows, you implement point solutions that solve immediate problems based on what your needs dictate. You continue to do this as your business grows until the complexity of all these bespoke systems becomes unmanageable.

Now you're a medium-sized business seeking simplicity and operational efficiency. You need to reduce your overheads in terms of the number of systems and the complexity. While you're too big for the plethora of point solutions, you're too small to have an internal technology capability that can support a level of complexity from best-of-breed solutions. Much like the crowded café kitchen, you're looking for versatility and simplicity – in our case, an ERP.

The mistake many medium-sized businesses make is not using the opportunity to reduce complexity. Ideally, you want to strike a balance. This means not trying to find a unicorn solution that does everything, but equally not investing in a litany of best-of-breed point solutions – because you simply don't have the capacity to manage the complexity. The time will come when you're a large business and can afford those types of tools. But right now, you want to aim for having the least number of systems possible, trading off specialisation for simplification. The only caveat is to make sure the tools are fit for purpose. While it might seem ideal to end up with one system to rule them all, the best approach is to buy tech to match your business's life stage. As an SME considering an ERP, just remember: fewer systems equals less overhead.

A Melbourne-based manufacturer of high-end tapware began as an online B2C retailer in the early 2000s. Over the course of 20 years, it grew to be a household name in premium tapware, sold through business-to-business relationships rather than direct-to-consumer. The various pivots and changes of the business saw the introduction of multiple systems, stitched together with a lot of manual processes. It's a fairly typical story for most high-growth SME businesses.

The challenge for the business now is that the complexity of those solutions, combined with the overhead of the manual processes to stitch the end-to-end business together, has become untenable and is prohibiting the business's growth. The technology strategy, therefore, is not to replace the multiple bespoke small business systems with multiple bespoke large business systems. Rather, it's to recognise that at their size, the best approach is to seek to simplify and achieve operational efficiencies. This will enable them to free up their people's time and focus on higher value activities to further grow the business.

# PART 2A

YOU AND
YOUR TEAM

MISTAKE
15

# The leader isn't all in

ONE OF THE greatest challenges of implementing any system in a business is when the decision maker, who's responsible for the outcome, doesn't fully lean in and lead by example. There's often this perception: 'I want the change, but I'm not willing to change.' Leaders expect all subordinates throughout the business to change the way they operate and adopt the new processes. However, they themselves expect to still receive the same reports in the same format and do things the way they've always done. As one seasoned ERP project manager pointed out: 'In my experience, businesses assume that investing a large sum of money will solve all their problems without fully understanding or being involved in the process.'

This pretty quickly comes apart, because if the person leading the charge isn't genuinely fully invested and isn't seen by their direct reports as living the talk, then their leadership team will generally apply the same ethos to their level of investment. This ends up permeating the business and undermining the investment. In his paper on organisational change, Jason A.

Hubbart found that when leaders fail to clearly communicate the reasons for change and don't ensure that employees understand and accept these reasons, it hinders the business's ability to grow, adapt, and improve. Without clear communication of vision, demonstration of expectations, and ensuring staff buy-in, employees are less likely to engage and support the initiative, ultimately hampering its success.

The best ERP implementation projects happen when leadership is all-in. They genuinely set a vision for the business, talk about the benefits they plan to get from the systems, and are actively involved in the change management. They actively engage with individuals across the company to understand their concerns, how it impacts their roles, and continue to set the tone. This helps everyone see how the new solution will help achieve overarching goals. Leaders actively participate in the training, and when the system goes live, they are there, doing their job day-to-day using the tools, rather than expecting someone else to do the work and just hand them reports.

Imagine a football team that's experiencing a performance slump. The season is in jeopardy and the coach's job is on the line. They have an all-team meeting and the players make it clear that they are unhappy with the coaching style. The coach lets them know that he's not happy with the way they are following the plays. If everyone buys into the change and the leader demonstrates that they are changing their coaching style, the team will follow suit. But if it's simply assumed that the players will lean in and do what's asked of them without demonstrated behavioural change from the coach, nothing happens.

To avoid this pitfall, leaders must fully commit to the change they wish to see in their organisation. They should actively participate in training, use the new systems daily, and consistently demonstrate the behaviours they expect from their teams. By doing so, leaders not only set the standard, but also inspire their teams to follow suit. This ensures a smoother and more successful implementation of new systems and processes.

In 2021, a confectionery manufacturer in New South Wales with 150 staff faced a colossal failure in their ERP implementation due to a lack of leadership buy-in. The CEO was enthusiastic about the new system but did not actively participate in the process. The project was handed off to middle management without clear direction or involvement from the top. This resulted in widespread confusion, resistance from staff, months of business interruption, and significant reputational damage, including the loss of two significant retail customers. The failure was so severe that the owners decided to remove the CEO.

An independent consultant was brought in for a post-implementation review, and the key finding was that senior leadership did not genuinely buy in.

A new CEO was selected with a specific mandate to engage with the wider workforce and leverage the lessons learned from the previous failure. The change management process was intensive, focusing on winning back the hearts and minds of the employees. The new CEO actively engaged from the start.

Occasionally, he'd turn up at smoko just to get a sense of the vibe on the shop floor and talk about his vision for the future. He also made a point of regularly attending and soliciting feedback through toolbox meetings. Importantly, he didn't lead from his office; he participated in system testing and training alongside the staff, literally working side by side with them. Despite the early challenges, the project was widely successful, demonstrating the critical importance of leadership buy-in for the successful implementation of new systems.

# Inadequate stakeholder involvement

ONE OF THE biggest mistakes people make in ERP projects is not having the right people in the tent.

This mistake happens because numerous groups of stakeholders need to be actively involved and engaged in the process, yet they often aren't. People are often said to be your greatest asset, but in the context of an ERP project, they can be both your greatest asset and your greatest weakness.

The first group you need to wrangle is your senior leadership team. These are the people responsible for the day-to-day operation of their part of the business and the only ones who can drive the behavioural change necessary for adopting a new ERP. Yet when they're brought into the tent, some managers will sit in the room, smile, and say, 'Yes, yes, yes, no problem, we'll take care of that,' but as soon as they walk out, they go straight to their direct reports and badmouth the project, the team, and the decisions. Kim Williams, who joined News Corp as CEO in 2011 after a decade at Foxtel, was not one to mince his words.

Not long into the job and faced with the task of a significant restructuring of the business, he made it abundantly clear that he wasn't interested in people smiling and agreeing with him in a room and then dissenting behind his back. He famously said he wouldn't be 'grin-fucked'.

In one notable case, a not-for-profit organisation based in Victoria, responsible for providing ready-to-eat meals to hundreds of thousands across Australia, faced severe challenges during its ERP implementation. Despite having the right system to support future growth, the project faltered due to a lack of stakeholder engagement and change management. Employees, especially those in operations and the warehouse, resisted the new system, preferring their old methods. Leadership failed to involve these critical stakeholders in the discovery and design phases, leading to a significant divide within the organisation.

A consultant hired to rescue the project highlighted the core issue, stating: 'They just did not have staff buy-in and ended up with this huge clunky process where they were worse off from where they started.' The emotional toll was significant, as many did not understand that the change was not a risk to their jobs but was crucial for scaling the business and serving more people in need. The consultant recalled, 'I've seen people literally in tears in front of me, saying, 'This is all I know. This is all I've done for 15 years of my life.' They were so resistant to the change because they feared it would eliminate their jobs.' He further emphasised, 'Management hadn't prepared staff for what was going to happen. Instead of seeing the new system as a tool to help them, they saw it as a threat.' The leadership failed to communicate that the system's purpose was not to reduce hours but to enhance efficiency so they could serve more people. In the end, the entire project was abandoned. A ridiculous amount of money was wasted that could have gone to helping people, and the organisation remained unable to scale to help the number of people they intended to.

The solution is to ensure everyone is on board and understands the vision. They need to know your why and your expectations. This begins with every manager, production manager, chief engineer, plant supervisor, and other senior leaders who are the champions of the project within their part of the business. They need to buy into it. Give them the opportunity to speak up and air their grievances and concerns, but they are not allowed to say no. They should absolutely voice their concerns so the project can address them, but you need to make it abundantly clear that you won't tolerate dissent. Dissent amongst your senior people will ensure failure within that part of the organisation. Those teams won't buy in because their leader won't drive them to do so. Your leaders need to make it particularly clear that the success of the project is paramount and that they want the team to help find ways to make it work, not just create barriers and complaints. Importantly, your leaders need to be sure that their people feel heard. Teams should be encouraged to raise concerns, but they need to do so proactively and productively with a view to success. It also doesn't mean it's an open invitation to push back on the change and raise what are not genuine concerns or challenges but rather thinly veiled attempts to maintain the status quo.

By fostering a culture of genuine engagement and proactive problem-solving, you can steer your ERP project to a successful implementation.

# Underestimating internal effort and setting unrealistic timelines

ALMOST EVERY SME that undertakes an ERP project inevitably falls into the trap of underestimating the effort required and setting unrealistic timelines.

It's understandable why this happens. Business leaders typically have not been through an ERP implementation before, so they have no reference point against which to estimate the effort required and the likely timelines. In a growing SME, most people are already at capacity, so there's a strong desire to reap the benefits as soon as possible to gain some operational efficiency. During the courting phase, software vendors and implementation partners have no incentive to temper your expectations or manage your ambition. They know if you were aware of how long and difficult the process would be, you might reconsider. It's in their best interest for you to believe the project can be completed quickly and with minimal effort.

Unfortunately, this often leads business owners to believe they can complete these projects in about 12 weeks, with just a few workshops, some training, and maybe some testing. While the steps are true, the amount of effort required is significantly more.

What ends up happening is that the people who best understand your business, the business processes and how the new processes will impact your business moving forward, don't get the requisite time to spend with the vendor. Any time they do dedicate tends to be in addition to their main responsibilities. In a business that is already thin on the ground, there isn't spare capacity waiting around. So, they focus on their day jobs. When their work hours are up, they don't have time to dedicate to the side project. As a result, the new processes are built into the system with limited information or the best intentions but without optimal design.

Often, what happens next is that you get towards the end of the implementation, around the testing phase, and issues start to surface. The go-live date keeps getting pushed out. Eventually, leadership draws a line in the sand and decides they are spending too much money and time. Research suggests that 90% of ERP implementations are late or over budget. Feeling the pressure to realise the benefits, leadership pick a date and commit to it. Everyone makes a last-ditch attempt to throw energy at the project to go live.

When the system goes live, all the challenges with the newly designed processes start to surface. People become less productive than they were before the system, and sentiment within the organisation dips significantly. Worse still, the only way to get value out of the new tool is to re-architect those processes and pay the vendor to re-implement them. So you end up paying twice for the implementation, plus you suffer a productivity deficit during the period when the system is not working efficiently. The lost sentiment among your staff makes it terribly difficult, even when the solution is fixed, for them to buy into adopting the new processes.

I find it helps to consider implementing an ERP like preparing for a marathon. Dedicated effort and steady progress will give you the best chance of success on race day. If you half-arse your preparation or leave your training to the 11th hour, best case, you won't be ready and will perform poorly; worst case, you'll injure yourself and won't be able to compete.

So, what should you do?

Firstly, assume your ERP project estimation skills are no better than your ability to nail a box trifecta on Cup day. We can't help but be optimistic when we start a project, so do yourself a favour and ask around. You'll know people who've done this before, and they'll be happy to tell you how much they under-cooked their estimate. Failing that, pick a timeline and add 30-50%. If you think it will take 12 weeks, it's safer – and more realistic – to plan for 18. You need time in your plan to accommodate for unforeseen challenges.

Secondly, dedicate someone in the organisation who will have no other job than to work with the vendor to ensure the system gets implemerted properly. You might call them project manager or business analyst, but I prefer to call them the platform owner. This perscn will coordinate all the meetings, ensure all your internal stakeholders are at the right sessions, make sure all the training is done properly, and ensure all testing is thorough, setting you up for success. At the end of your project, you'll end up with someone who intimately understands the solution and is the champion for it within your business – a subject matter expert who can help your people leverage the best from the solution.

Thirdly, all your key folks need dedicated time to be involved in the relevant parts of the project. This means it can't be an additional duty on top of their day jobs. You need to figure out how to reassign work to free them up or backfill their roles for periods so they can be involved in everything from early-stage discovery and the design of the new processes, to the design of training and especially thorough testing.

# Selecting the wrong time of year for an implementation

ONE OF THE mistakes manufacturing businesses often make when implementing an ERP system is choosing the wrong time of year for the go-live. This can be influenced by various factors, including the availability of implementation partner resources, but the result is often going live at the worst possible time for the business.

Manufacturers often forget that key people are needed throughout the process. I've spoken to many project managers whose implementations went wrong because someone forgot to ensure that the supervisors were all available during the go-live. The most experienced people on the factory floor were on leave when they were trying to manage multiple shifts of people doing training and running systems in parallel.

An ERP implementation is a little bit like coordinating a music festival. There's no perfect time to run a music festival, but you plan for the best weather, consider other festivals that might compete for attendees, manage artist fatigue, and ensure you're working around the availability of your international headline act.

In your business, you face similar challenges. Think about the mad rush to get everything out the door before the Christmas break. The manufacturing floor is flat out, but it's often quiet upstairs in the back office because the admin staff at your suppliers and customers are all off at Christmas parties, not necessarily sending through invoices. When July and August roll around, your manufacturing may slow down, but your back office is flat out doing end-of-year finances and performance reviews.

Neglecting to plan around these cycles can lead to significant issues. Key personnel may be unavailable, training sessions can be rushed, and the business may struggle to maintain normal operations during the transition. This can result in operational disruptions, increased costs, and employee dissatisfaction.

In 2023, a precision machining manufacturer based in southeast Queensland, employing 130 staff, faced a significant issue during their ERP implementation. The company planned to go live in August, aiming to coincide with a typically slow period in their production schedule. However, their foreman, a long-time and well-respected employee, was scheduled for long service leave and had booked a family holiday to Europe. Despite this, the vendor convinced them to proceed with the go-live due to their own availability, promising on-site support. Initially, the transition seemed smooth, but the foreman's absence soon caused major problems. Factory floor staff struggled with the new system, as the rushed training sessions left many confused and frustrated. This dissatisfaction escalated quickly, leading to union involvement, with complaints about inadequate training and poor timing. The union's intervention turned the situation into a significant conflict, while operational disruptions led to missed production deadlines and increased costs. Despite the vendor's on-site presence, their support was insufficient, and without their foreman, the company found itself in crisis mode, managing both the ERP transition and union disputes.

**So what can you do about it?**

To ensure a successful ERP implementation, consider the following steps:

1. **Plan Ahead**: Start planning at least six months in advance. This gives you ample time to manage leave schedules and ensure that all key personnel will be available during the go-live period.

2. **Stagger the Implementation**: Consider delivering the project in phases. For instance, you could handle data migration, training, and go-live for your back office and finance teams during December when it's typically quieter for them. Then, progressively build, test, and train for the manufacturing floor go-live in the new year when it's quieter for that department.

3. **Communicate Effectively**: Maintain regular communication with all stakeholders throughout the project. Establish a communication plan that outlines how and when updates will be shared. This might include weekly status meetings, bi-weekly progress emails, and a dedicated project dashboard accessible to all team members.

4. **Involve Key Personnel**: Ensure that key personnel are involved in the planning and implementation stages. This includes supervisors, experienced factory floor staff, and other critical team members who will use the ERP system daily.

5. **Schedule Training Sessions Carefully**: Plan training sessions at times when key users are available and can focus without the pressure of peak work periods. Avoid scheduling training during known busy times or when key staff are on leave.

6. **Monitor and Adjust**: Keep an eye on the implementation process and be prepared to adjust your plans if necessary. Flexibility can help you address any unexpected issues that arise during the project.

PART 2B

THE FINAL
GRIND: MAKE
OR BREAK

# Failing to do your housekeeping

PROBABLY THE ACHILLES heel for every ERP implementation ends up being data migration. The mistake is that senior leaders don't appreciate the value of getting this right or the effort involved. They under-resource it and mess it up.

This mistake happens because data migration is incredibly hard to do. Many leaders falsely assume that putting in a new system automatically means you're going to get fantastic data. They don't understand that without proper attention, 'shit in, shit out' will prevail.

The first issue is not understanding what data is valuable and necessary in the new system. This leads to misconceptions around data requirements. Often, you get half-assed or ill-informed perspectives about the need for data migration. Statements like, 'Oh, I think we need to keep that for seven years,' are often based on half-truths and scuttlebutt. Even when the legislation being quoted is accurate, what's required to be kept is pretty specific. However, it's generally and incorrectly painted with a broad brush across everything, so what ends up happening is a lot of useless data gets migrated at a significant cost.

An analogy that might help here is moving house. When you're moving, you typically have a good clean-out of all the things in your cupboards, drawers and closets, and throw out stuff that you're not going to need in the new house. You then pack everything carefully and label the boxes. You don't waste effort and money bringing over stuff that you don't need. Because you've taken the time upfront to determine what makes sense to bring across, and it's been carefully packed and accurately labelled, you know exactly which room it's going to go into when everything lands at the other side. You know where it is, and you know it's going to be where it's supposed to be. This is exactly the same with data migration in an ERP project.

Another significant mistake is having an ill-considered strategy around how you're going to cleanse the data. One of the traps some businesses fall into is giving the data migration task to a low-level employee or a temp – someone with zero vested interest in getting it right and who is not being paid enough to care. If the data is critical for your organisation and you're going to rely on it for reporting and forecasting, you really want to make sure the person doing it has your back. A university grad or a temp who is begrudgingly keying data into the system doesn't really care if it's inaccurate because there's no consequence to them.

The consequences to the business of failing to do housekeeping can be catastrophic.

A classic case study is when Target tried to expand from North America into Canada with an aggressive timeline to get multiple stores live. For whatever reason, they decided not to use the ERP solution that the North American business was using but to implement the SAP solution. Their migration strategy was not to extract and cleanse data from the existing solutions but to manually key 75 000 products into the system. Better still, some genius decided it was a good idea to get a bunch of low-level employees to key in the information. The result was, by expert estimates, 30% accuracy in the data. It absolutely killed their supply chain, and they lost millions of dollars. In the end, they pulled out of the Canadian market altogether.

If you don't handle this properly, you will face significant issues. I don't know how many times I've seen ERPs get either to the testing phase or go-live before someone realises there are fundamental problems with the system, all of which boil down to the system doing exactly what it's told with the rubbish data it's been fed.

The third mistake is not allocating enough time and resources for this task. This is a laborious task, and it can't be something that somebody does while they're watching Netflix or on the side while also trying to run payroll and other things. Data cleansing requires hyper-focus and attention to detail. The only way to get through it is to dedicate the time and resources to get it right.

So how do we do this right?

First, take stock of what data you *actually need* and what will work in the new system. Studies have shown that 'Organisations usually have a plethora of data in legacy systems. The problem is that this data might not be compatible with the new ERP system.' Determining what you bring across doesn't necessarily mean only what you're obligated to keep; it also means key operational data within your organisation that is crucial to your day-to-day and makes sense to migrate to a new system. Trying to blindly migrate everything you have is probably going to have limited value, and will cost a significant amount of money and time.

Second, have a *clear strategy* for cleansing the data. Make sure the person doing it has your back. You don't want a low-level employee or a temp who doesn't care about the accuracy of the data.

Third, allocate *enough time and resources*. Data cleansing requires hyper-focus and attention to detail. Dedicate the time and resources necessary to get it right.

Finally, test thoroughly. Research has shown that 'Stress testing must be performed before going live. What works in small volumes does not necessarily work when put under the operational loads of a live environment.' If we're talking about financial information, run the old and new systems in parallel and do month-ends for one or more financial quarters to ensure both systems are producing the same numbers. Do not go live if you haven't got the data right.

By following this structured approach, you can significantly improve the chances of a successful ERP implementation and avoid the costly mistakes that can arise from a poor data migration strategy.

# Insufficient or inappropriate training

IT MIGHT SEEM obvious, but since it so often goes awry, I'll just say it: training is a crucial element for the success and growth of any business. Despite this seemingly obvious fact, there remain a few common challenges that businesses face when it comes to effective training that result in a less-than-ideal ERP implementation.

Firstly, many business leaders view training as a cost rather than an investment, and seek to minimise this 'cost'. Secondly, they mistakenly believe that training is a one-time event rather than an ongoing process that evolves with your business. Thirdly, they often fail to meet their employees where they are, not considering the varied needs and learning styles within their teams. Lastly, the implementation project team creates a team of 'super users' or subject matter experts who are expected to train the teams but don't have the necessary supporting processes.

### An Investment vs. a Cost

Taking people out of their day jobs inevitably impacts production and incurs significant costs. So many business leaders view training as a cost rather than an investment. Seeking to minimise this 'cost', business leaders often reduce the amount of effort they put into training their people, unwittingly sabotaging the success and potential future growth delivered by getting the implementation right. It won't be right if people don't understand how their daily lives change, why the new way is better, how to get the most efficiency and information out of the new tools, and how to remain productive.

### Training is Not a One-Time Event

Another common mistake businesses make is preparing their team for the initial go-live, but neglecting to put in place an ongoing training capability for staff. This mistake happens because while there's a lot of excitement and investment of time during the implementation phase, priorities quickly change. What was well-intentioned follow-through largely devolves to training via osmosis, where people learn on the job by looking over the shoulder of the person they're working with. Inevitably, this results in a game of Chinese whispers where someone's interpretation of what they were told, combined with shortcuts they have created, gets passed to the next person as the way it's done. Rather than learning the correct process, the new employee gets the equivalent of 'This isn't what we were told, but it works pretty well for me,' and the quality of that training degrades over time, introducing errors in processes and data.

Often well-intentioned folks who have been taught incorrectly end up using processes that lead to errors. These errors don't get picked up for a significant period, impacting your numbers, forecasting and operational efficiency. The reality is that people in your business will move around and take on different roles over time, and as they move, there will be a requirement to train them on various new parts of the system and business processes. Similarly, people will leave your business, and their replacements will need training.

### *Everyone Learns Differently*

Businesses often fail to meet their employees where they are, not considering the varied needs and learning styles within their teams. This happens because project teams, also struggling with time, cost and capability constraints, adopt a one-size-fits-all approach to training.

This invariably fails because the analytical folks in your finance department have very different needs and learning styles compared to the folks on the factory floor. The approach doesn't consider that some folks will respond really well to video tutorials, others will need hands-on instruction, and some will be happy with just a written Standard Operating Procedure (SOP).

### Superusers Without Support

Another common training mistake is when businesses set up superusers, but neglect to support that group with multimodal training. These superusers are expected to train others on top of their day jobs, which leads to insufficient time dedicated to either role. Superusers should be there to support people who have been through training, to answer questions and clarify understanding, rather than be a substitute for training the teams.

If you really want to do your implementation justice, think about launching your ERP just like you would think about launching a new product. Imagine your team comes up with a brilliant new product idea that you think will revolutionise the industry and win significant market share. You wouldn't just design it and then put it out on the market. When you launch your product, you'll have comprehensive user manuals, demonstrations and customer support to ensure that your customers understand and can effectively use the product. If you didn't do this and released the product without any guidance, your customers would end up confused, frustrated and likely give up on your product, wasting your investment in R&D and bringing the product to market. The time and effort that you spend with your team training them is akin to the resources spent on marketing and customer education for your new product. Both are investments that ensure your success. Without them, even the best-designed product or system can fail because end-users don't know how to use it effectively. Well-educated customers can become loyal advocates for your product, just as well-trained employees can drive productivity, efficiency and growth within your company. Initial investment in training ensures that the system is not just implemented but utilised to its full potential.

My advice for avoiding these mistakes is to invest in training as though it were directly tied to revenue, implement a continuous training program, meet people where they are in terms of learning style, and set your subject matter experts up for success.

Reframing training as an investment highlights the long-term benefits and ensures that the system is implemented and utilised to its full potential. Continuous training programs ensure that as people move around and take on new roles, or as new people join the business, they are adequately trained. Meeting people where they are involves using a variety of training methods to cater to different learning styles and needs. Investment in multimodal training like videos, standard operating procedures, face-to-face training and train-the-trainer models will ensure long-term success with benefits outweighing costs. Create a team of subject matter experts representing different roles across the organisation. They should receive extra training and can support their colleagues to clarify and implement the new processes and tools they've learned.

**Expert tip!** – Always schedule training first thing in the morning when your team are fresh; not immediately after lunch when the food coma sets in.

# Inadequate testing

EARLIER, I REFERRED to data quality and housekeeping as the Achilles heel of ERP implementations. However, ERP projects face another critical weakness: inadequate testing. Inadequate testing can be equally detrimental, making it one of the most serious mistakes that can undermine an ERP project.

When I reached out to my network of peers for horror stories about ERP implementations to be included in this book, the overwhelming majority pointed to inadequate testing as the primary reason their projects failed. They emphasised that their testing efforts were either insufficient or improperly conducted, leading to significant issues post-implementation.

It's impossible to overstate the amount and importance of thorough testing throughout the ERP implementation. Just think about some of the more obvious tests you're going to need to do. You want to make sure that you're running multiple trials of your end-of-month and end-of-year processes in parallel with the current system to ensure the numbers line up. You need to test your inventory management capabilities to ensure that when you're barcode scanning inventory, it's actually going to the right place and that you're not double-counting or undercounting. You want to make sure that time sheet data flows correctly through to your activity-based costing and cost of goods sold calculations. I'm only just scratching the surface of the obvious ones, and these alone could take weeks of testing.

The other thing that's super important to realise is that testing is not just a final step done at the end of your project; it should be an ongoing process throughout the project. Continuous testing, reviewing, and adjusting are crucial to ensure your ERP system performs flawlessly when it goes live.

To try and drive this point home, I trawled through the numerous case studies shared by my peers for this book. In the end, I decided not to shame any particular person. Instead, let's reflect on one of the biggest ClustERPuck's in the world: NIKE's i2 implementation.

In 2000, Nike decided to implement i2's demand-planning software as part of its ambitious strategy to create a single integrated database for its supply chain management. Nike's leadership team believed that i2's predictive algorithms would revolutionise their supply chain and streamline operations across its global network. However, the reality was far from the vision.

The software, plagued with bugs and integration issues, misfired badly. It over-ordered thousands of unpopular sneakers while under-ordering the highly popular Air Jordans. Orders were either duplicated or deleted, and the demand planner would erase ordering data after a few weeks, making it impossible to track what had been requested. The critical oversight was not testing how well the software integrated with Nike's existing systems, and not running enough real-world tests to see how the software would handle actual demand.

The consequences of these testing oversights were severe. Nike experienced a 20 per cent drop in its stock price, and copped a bunch of class-action lawsuits. The misalignment in product orders disrupted Nike's inventory and supply chain, leading to $100m in lost sales and substantial repetitional damage. Roland Wolfram, Nike's vice president of global operations and technology, famously referred to the i2 debacle as 'the poster child for failed implementations' and Nike's chairman, president, and CEO, Phil Knight, famously lamented, 'This is what you get for $400 million, huh?'

This situation highlights the critical importance of thorough and continuous testing throughout the ERP project lifecycle, ensuring that all components function correctly *before* going live.

So now I'm assuming you're convinced that when you're embarking on your ERP journey you need to crack the whip on your team and your ERP provider to get the testing planning up to scratch. You might be asking what should you be asking for? Well, a lot! But for sake of time, here's 10 critical types of testing – it's not exhaustive, but it's a good starting point.

### Data Quality Testing

- Verify that all data is correctly migrated from the old system to the new ERP system.
- Ensure data accuracy, completeness and consistency.

### Process Testing

- Test new business processes to ensure they are correctly implemented and functional.
- Validate workflows and make sure they align with business requirements.

### User Acceptance Testing (UAT)

- Involve end-users in testing the system to ensure it meets their needs and is user-friendly.
- Identify any issues or discrepancies from a user perspective.
- UAT is your opportunity to shake down the effectiveness of your training. If your team doesn't know the software, then **don't go live!**

### Integration Testing

- Ensure that the ERP system integrates seamlessly with other existing systems, such as Customer Relationship Management (CRM), Supply Chain Management (SCM), and Manufacturing Execution Systems (MES).
- Test data flow between systems to verify that interfaces work correctly.

**Performance Testing**

- ◆ Assess the system's performance under various conditions and workloads.
- ◆ Identify any bottlenecks or performance issues.

**Security Testing**

- ◆ Test the ERP system for vulnerabilities and ensure it complies with security standards.
- ◆ Verify that user roles and permissions are correctly implemented.

**Regression Testing (after any changes or updates)**

- ◆ Test the ERP system to ensure existing functionalities are not affected.
- ◆ Continuously retest to maintain system integrity.

**Training and Simulation Testing**

- ◆ Conduct thorough training sessions and simulations for staff to use the system.
- ◆ Ensure that users are comfortable with the system and can perform their tasks effectively.

**End-to-End Testing**

- ◆ Test the entire workflow from start to finish to ensure that all components of the ERP system work together correctly.
- ◆ Validate the overall business process flow.

**Parallel Testing**

- ◆ Run the new ERP system alongside the old system to compare results and ensure accuracy.
- ◆ Verify that financial reports, inventory management, and other critical operations match expected outcomes.

Each of these testing types is essential to ensure that the ERP system is implemented smoothly, functions correctly, and meets the business's needs without disrupting operations.

# So, what do we do now?

IF YOU'VE REACHED this point and thought, 'Crikey, that's a lot of things to consider,' then you're right. Unfortunately, this isn't even a definitive list, so if you're feeling nervous or uncomfortable, that's to be expected. My goal isn't to scare you out of taking action, but to open your eyes to the complexity and provide assurance that ClustERPucks are avoidable. I hope you'll find that the lessons and tools I've provided will help you navigate these challenges with confidence and seize the opportunities that lie ahead.

So, let's say you're feeling ready for the journey. Let me paint a picture of what that's going to look like.

On this graph, we have two lines. They represent the growth trajectory of your business with your current technology stack. The first line is the amount of effort you need to put in as a business to get returns. The second line is your productivity. At this point, they are largely following the same trajectory and are mostly flat because you've already highlighted that the technology in your business is no longer serving you.

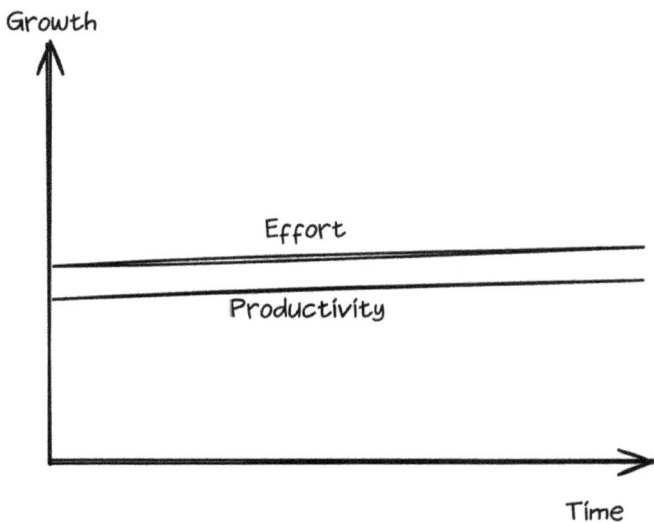

Growth

Effort

Productivity

Time

When you embark on your ERP project, the graph changes. There's a period where the amount of effort you need to put in as an organisation will significantly increase. That's the period between kicking off your journey and starting to reap the benefits. All the steps we've discussed through the book, from understanding requirements to building, testing, deploying and managing change, are all high-effort activities. Meanwhile, your productivity line will drop below where it typically is.

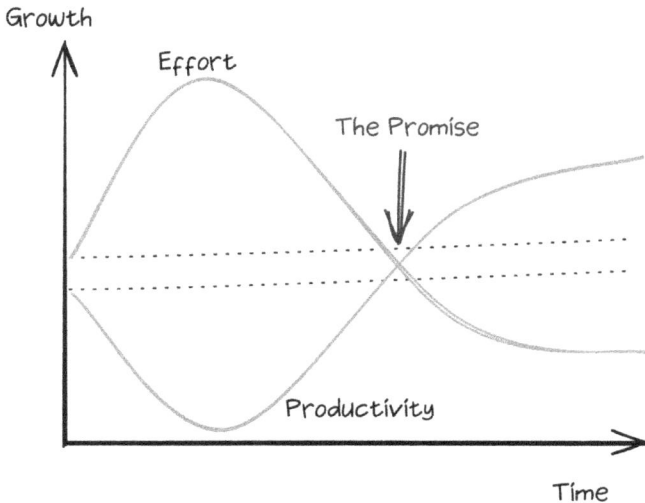

Growth

Effort

The Promise

Productivity

Time

The promise is that once everything is sorted and your ERP is delivering value, these two lines cross, and you'll end up in a scenario where, for less effort, you have more productivity. This is the point when your ERP investment pays off. But it's the initial period, where the two lines diverge, that is the most painful part of the process. This is ClustERPuck territory.

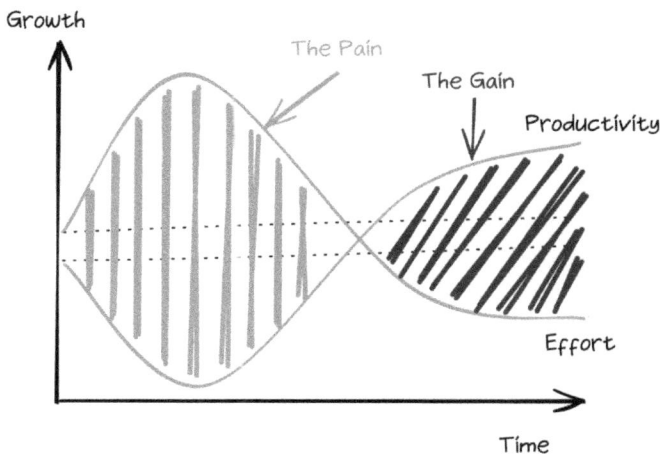

This part is hard because lots of things need to happen that are over and above our day jobs. It requires a lot of focus, but without support, people get distracted, cut corners, or miss critical elements. Without the experience of those who know how to navigate this difficult time, there are few directions our journey can take. What typically happens is either we give up and waste all the money and time invested, or we push through the pain to go live but never achieve the productivity gain, carrying the tax of the mistakes we made along the way. Essentially, we end up in a worse situation – a ClustERPuck.

However, with the right support, this journey can look very different. With my help, you'll have a clear roadmap and the benefit of experience to guide you. This means fewer distractions, better focus and the ability to anticipate and avoid critical pitfalls. Instead of cutting corners, you'll make informed decisions that keep the project on track. The productivity line will start rising sooner, and the effort required will be managed effectively. The result? A successful ERP implementation that delivers real value, maximises productivity and ensures that your investment pays off. You'll avoid the common mistakes and emerge with a system that truly supports your business growth.

I can introduce you to plenty of folks who've been on this journey and made it a success. What gets me out of bed every morning is helping people like you make this process as painless, successful and cost-effective as possible. Most business leaders can't afford the time, cost, or personal reputational damage of presiding over a ClustERPuck. So, if you've read this book and feel like you need support to navigate these challenges in your context, I am here to help.

Let's guide your business to a better future where growth is sustainable, because you have the right tools and processes in place to get you there. I want to help you make confident decisions and navigate through the short-term pain in such a way that you actually get the long-term gain. You don't have to face these challenges alone. Seeking help is a sign of strong leadership and a step towards ensuring your ERP implementation is a success. If that sounds like a conversation you want to have, please reach out. Let's work together to achieve the success your business deserves.

Ready to take the next steps?

Visit **www.shanewilliams.com.au/clusterpuck** for a full range of resources to guide your ERP journey.

### Shout-outs

Putting this book together has been like a good session at the pub – full of stories, laughs, and hard-earned lessons. I couldn't have done it without the legends who shared their yarns, trusting me to keep their identities under wraps. Even though your names aren't here, your 'off-the-record' stories have brought real depth and character to these pages. Special thanks also to my clients, who not only allowed me to share some of their experiences but also connected me with many of the contributors. Without your input, this book would be just another boring manual. Instead, it's a collection of real-life screw-ups and victories that will hopefully save others from a few headaches. I'm honoured to have been entrusted with your stories.

Special thanks to my cheer squad – the folks who leaned in and pushed me to get this book done. To Col Fink for challenging my procrastination and pushing me to get a first draft out. To Sophie Krantz, Monique Richardson, Katie Rees, and Mark Butler for getting me back on the wagon when I got in my own way. To Bob Sudharshan for the daily encouragement to keep going. To Nanneth Celebre, my research assistant, for your invaluable support throughout this journey. And to Paul Mason, my co-host on Manufacturing Tech Australia Podcast, for doing the heavy lifting for the show while I was in book mode.

And last but not least, thanks (once again) to my family for persevering with the missed weekends and the endless late nights.

So, here's to all of you – *cheers*!

# References

Abd Elmonem, M. A., Nasr, E. S., & Geith, M. H. (2016). Benefits and challenges of cloud ERP systems — A systematic literature review. *Future Computing and Informatics Journal*, 1(1-2), 1–9. https://doi.org/10.1016/j.fcij.2017.03.003

Castaldo, J. (2016). The last days of Target: The untold tale of Target Canada's difficult birth, tough life and brutal death. *Canadian Business*. Retrieved May 29, 2024, from https://canadianbusiness.com/ideas/the-last-days-of-target-canada/

Ezer, J. (2017). Are software salesmen dirty? *Huffington Post*. Retrieved May 29, 2024, from https://www.huffpost.com/entry/are-software-salesmen-dir_b_579181

Grossman, T., & Walsh, J. (2004). Avoiding the pitfalls of ERP system implementation. *Information Systems Management*, 21(2), 38–42. https://doi.org/10.1201/1078/44118.21.2.20040301/80420.6

Hubbart, J. A. (2023). Organizational change: Considering truth and buy-in. *Administrative Sciences*, 13(1), 3. https://doi.org/10.3390/admsci13010003

Koch, C. (2004). Nike rebounds: How Nike recovered from its supply chain disaster. *CIO*. Retrieved May 29, 2024, from https://www.cio.com/article/264637/enterprise-resource-planning-nike-rebounds-how-nike-recovered-from-its-supply-chain-disaster.html

O'Leary, D. E. (2000). *Enterprise resource planning systems: Systems, life cycle, electronic commerce, and risk.* Cambridge University Press.

Saade, R. G., & Nijher, H. (2016). Critical success factors in enterprise resource planning implementation. *Journal of Enterprise Information Management, 29*(1), 72–96. https://doi.org/10.1108/jeim-03-2014-0028

Venkatraman, S., & Fahd, K. (2016). Challenges and success factors of ERP systems in Australian SMEs. *Systems, 4*(2), 20. https://doi.org/10.339C/systems4020020

# Praise for *ClustERPuck*

Shane brings his sleeves-rolled-up, good-humoured approach to this book, offering clear, practical insights for business leaders navigating the complex world of ERP implementations. He distils years of hands-on experience into a straightforward guide, helping companies avoid the costly mistakes many still make. Whether you're just starting your ERP journey or looking to improve an ongoing project, *ClustERPuck* provides the critical knowledge you need to make informed decisions and ensure success. Shane's real-world advice could be the difference between a smooth transformation and a disruptive failure.

**– Hakon Andersson, Head of Technology - Retail, Wesfarmers Health**

The world of ERP systems, IT, and AI moves so fast that, especially in today's demanding and competitive business environment, trying to stay ahead feels impossible when you're running a complex business. *ClustERPuck* really stands out because it cuts through all the jargon. It's written in a way that anyone can understand, even if you're not a technology expert. If I were selecting a new ERP system today, I'd reach for this book to ensure I make informed decisions and keep the focus on what's best for the business, not the vendor.

**– Tom Atherton, CEO, A.E. Atherton & Sons**

A brilliant, no-nonsense guide for manufacturers looking to avoid costly ERP mistakes. *ClustERPuck* distils years of experience into practical insights, helping you sidestep common pitfalls and make smarter decisions. Perfect for busy leaders, this book provides a clear roadmap to success. Shane Williams' expertise is evident in the thoughtful structure and actionable tips.

**– Ishan Galapathy, Operational Excellence Strategist, Speaker & Author**

As an SME business mentor, I have seen plenty of *ClustERPuck* examples of software implementation gone terribly wrong. As I read this book, I found myself nodding in furious agreement as scenario after scenario of real-life implementation horror stories were relived through these pages. Shane is an expert in how to avoid these incredibly expensive and time-consuming nightmares. His practical advice is written in plain language, easy to read and invaluable. Don't even think about implementing an ERP system without having read this book.

**—Chris Green, Managing Director, GYB Regional**


*ClustERPuck* is a must-read for any business navigating the complex world of ERP systems. Shane's candid, no-nonsense approach highlights the frequent misalignment between ERP salespeople and customers, often exacerbated by the fact that customers themselves may not fully understand their own needs. Having grown my manufacturing business from a one-person operation to over 50 staff across multiple locations, I wish I'd had this book ten years ago. It could have saved me a lot of money and countless frustrating hours. Shane's insights are invaluable for anyone looking to scale or streamline their systems. Thank you, Shane, for this exceptional guide!

**—Jack Fitzgerald, Founder & CTO, Think Manufacturing**


In my work with purpose-driven leaders, we often face the challenge of outgrown systems. Maintaining service levels that align with the brand while keeping costs viable makes integrated system upgrades a priority. Leading these efforts requires a distinct focus, separate from core business success. Just as a runner turns to a swim coach when transitioning to triathlons, discerning leaders seek expert guidance. Shane's forthright style and clear advice are exactly what's needed. I'll be sharing *ClustERPuck* with leaders who see enterprise system development as key to keeping their businesses fit for purpose.

**—Bernie Kelly, Transformation Partner**

Informative, practical and entertaining, Shane speaks to all levels of a business embarking on an ERP implementation. For those who have had their own *ClustERPuck*, you will find wisdom through reflection on lessons learned, and for those new to the journey you will benefit from the lived experience of others. A must-read for your leadership team and all stakeholders so that your collective efforts maximise the productivity benefits available to your business.

**– Nick Gray, CFO, CG&C Group**

*ClustERPuck* is a game-changer for anyone involved in ERP management. Shane's candid insights will guide you towards a smoother and more successful deployment. This book is a must-read for anyone looking to avoid costly misadventures and ensure their ERP journey is a success. I wish I'd had it 30 years ago when we started!

**– Leigh Pike, Chief Operations Officer, A.E. Atherton & Sons**

*ClustERPuck* is a masterclass in the no-nonsense approach to implementing ERP systems in small enterprises. From planning to execution, Shane cuts through jargon and delivers practical, actionable advice. The relatable writing style feels like a conversation with someone who's been through the trenches. The real-world case studies are invaluable, and you can tell the lessons come from actual experience, not theory. It's a must-read for anyone serious about getting real value from their ERP system and avoiding costly mistakes.

**– Jason van Lint, CTO, DIYBlinds**

Imagine you're sitting by a fire with one of your smartest, funniest friends, hearing horror stories about ERP implementations. Slowly, you realise the fire is fuelled by burning piles of corporate cash spent on those projects. Your friend leans in and says, 'Mate, you're about to make the same mistake.' That's the tone of *ClustERPuck*. ERP systems are confusing, and poorly done implementations are so hit-and-miss that you might as well blow that money on a piñata filled with regret. Williams tells you how to get it right in a relatable, irreverent, and funny way. You'll be glad you read it before it's your cash on the line.

**– Alex Hagan, Futurist, alexhagan.co**

Shane's straight-up pointers and high-vis warnings provide the perfect primer for change teams and senior managers who are about to undertake what is generally a white-knuckle ride for any organisation.

— Brook Thomas, GM Technology, McColl's Transport

In *ClustERPuck*, Shane gets straight to the heart of the painful issues in ERP implementations with his candid, no-bullshit approach. He lays out practical shortcuts that lead to success in these challenging digital transformations. For mid-market businesses, implementing ERP is a strategic necessity, and Shane's decades of experience shine through in the practical wisdom and nuanced insights he shares. With the help of this book, those new to digital transformation are far less likely to make costly mistakes. Shane champions real outcomes, setting you up for ERP success every step of the way.

— Michael Meyer, Founder & CEO, M31 Consulting

*ClustERPuck* isn't like most business books you've read. Shane cuts through the corporate jargon and tells it like it is – in plain, sometimes blunt, language. It's essential for anyone involved in an ERP replacement, from the C-suite sponsor all the way down. On every page, I recognised familiar issues, from vendor selection criteria to poor internal resourcing and weak data strategies. The message is clear: there's no substitute for hard work. By reading this book, you give yourself the best chance of ensuring that hard work pays off.

— Caspar Deman, Commercial Director, Central Innovation

Think ERP is just a walk in the park? Think again. The graveyard of failed system implementations is full of business leaders who thought they could delegate and skate by - only to find out the hard way that it is a beast of complexity. Year after year, they underestimate it and pay dearly. Shane's no-nonsense approach might feel like a punch to the gut, but trust me, the wisdom packed into *ClustERPuck* will save you time, money, and maybe even your career. Read it, learn it, and thank him later.

— Taural Rhoden – Managing Director, Accel Digital

*ClustERPuck* is packed with simple, practical tips that make a real difference. After 30 years of working in ERP implementation, I can say these are the things we deal with every day. If it's your first or even second time tackling ERP, this book will help you see what can go wrong and how to handle it. It's a must-read for anyone wanting to understand the ERP Implementation process.

**– Dianne Semmens, Managing Director, Acacia Consulting Services**

As a systems integrator helping businesses through ERP selection and implementation, it was refreshing to see Shane's take on the process. *ClustERPuck* breaks down ERP selection into clear, actionable steps, helping readers understand what to look for and what to avoid. I highly recommend this book to anyone in SME manufacturing who needs to make the critical decision of choosing the right ERP system.

**– Jon O'Brien, Managing Director ANZ, InfoConsulting**

A great read with real-life experiences and advice to help businesses navigate the treacherous evolution of systems and ERP. Shane's approach is a breath of fresh air, underlining the need for everyone's commitment to ensure a successful ERP implementation. Any business making mission-critical decisions should read *ClustERPuck* before diving into an ERP journey.

**– Michael Pendred, Managing Director, Stratus Group**

*ClustERPuck* just makes so much sense. In my 28-year supply-chain consulting career I've seen too many ERP implementations where the cost of business losses during implementation exceeded the ERP cost itself. And if you think you're too smart or experienced to get it wrong, think again - as Shane points out, the big brands have made costly mistakes too. This is a great read that's accessible to everyone, from the warehouse manager to the customer service admin team and is immeasurably valuable to the CIO and their team.

**– Peter Jones, Founder and Director, Prological**

Shane's no-nonsense, 'chewing the fat' style makes *ClustERPuck* an intuitive read that expertly covers the minefield of using ERP to meaningfully scale a small to medium enterprise. Drawing from real-life business case studies, Shane clearly demonstrates how each step of his ERP plan is designed to avoid the pitfalls of poor implementation and rollout, which could leave your business losing staff, customers, and market share alike.

**— Jason Purvis, Director, The OT Group**

Selecting an ERP is one of the most daunting tasks for any business owner or manager. You spend days wading through the BS, with everyone promising the world and telling you what you want to hear, but finding the right solution is still a real challenge. The ERP must improve what you do - otherwise, why spend the money? In *ClustERPuck*, Shane shares his experience and that of others to help you avoid the pitfalls and ensure your choice drives real business improvement. This wisdom is priceless and could save you a lot of time and money if followed.

**— Peter Smith, CEO, Boomaroo Nurseries**

*ClustERPuck* is a comprehensive guide that expertly navigates ERP implementation challenges, providing real-world case studies on common failures. Shane delivers practical insights to save time, money, and headaches for anyone embarking on an ERP or software platform implementation journey.

**— Paul Mason, Manufacturing Tech Australia**

*ClustERPuck* (love the name!) is a must-read for small and medium enterprises in the 'grow up' phase, aspiring to scale. It provides practical guidance on ERP implementation, emphasising crucial elements often overlooked in the process. In non-techy terms, Shane makes complex concepts easy to understand. This easy-to-read guide ensures your ERP implementation not only meets current needs but is also future-proofed for sustainable growth.

**— Nicola Harrop, Hourglass Business Analytics**

You know how stressed you feel when you finally need a new phone - new hardware, new features, AI to configure, different contracts, a new operating system, remembering passwords, connecting clouds, configuring security, migrating data, and then adding and updating apps? Multiply that by 1 million and you get the feeling of how scary buying and implementing expensive ERP software is - 100% core to the success of your business. Reading Shane's new book *ClustERPuck* is like having a trusted, worldly friend sit next to you while you upgrade - gifting you the wisdom of years of experience on what to do (and not to do!). Nobody in their right mind would turn down that help, or this book.

**– Nigel Dalton, Social Scientist, Reformed CIO and ERP Buyer**


One thing about us Aussies - we're a no-BS culture. We can sniff out nonsense, but sometimes we don't know what we don't know. Most SME manufacturers are top-notch at making things but might be clueless when it comes to implementing a world-class ERP that boosts real net profit. Enter Shane Williams. He's sliced through the *ClustERPuck*s of the industry to deliver straight-up, no-BS advice that'll save you time, money, and perhaps your hairline. This book will educate, equip, and empower you to navigate the IT minefield. Do yourself a favour - make the investment. You won't regret it.

**– Nathanael (Nato) Small, Leadership Adviser and Founder, Work2Live**

# About the Author

**Shane Williams** is a seasoned technology strategist with decades of experience in helping businesses streamline their operations through effective technology implementations. With master's degrees in both IT and business management, and extensive hands-on experience, Shane has led numerous successful projects, turning chaotic systems into efficient, productive workflows.

As a strategic technology advisor for manufacturing businesses, Shane specialises in maximising value from Software-as-a-Service (SaaS) platforms. He is the author of "The Platform Owners Guidebook: How Industry Experts Unlock Value from Enterprise Software" and the host of the podcasts "Manufacturing Tech Australia" and "Platform Diaries."

A sought-after speaker and advisor, Shane combines deep technical knowledge with practical insights, making complex concepts accessible and actionable. When not immersed in enabling his clients' businesses to scale, Shane enjoys craft beer, heavy-metal music, good coffee, motorcycle riding, and watching live sport.

9 780645 161724